THE COMING APOSTASY

EXPOSING THE SABOTAGE OF CHRISTIANITY FROM WITHIN

THE COMING APOSTASY

MARK HITCHCOCK
JEFF KINLEY

TYNDALE
MOMENTUM™

The nonfiction imprint of
Tyndale House Publishers, Inc.

Visit Tyndale online at www.tyndale.com.

Vist Tyndale Momentum online at www.tyndalemomentum.com.

TYNDALE, Tyndale Momentum, and Tyndale's quill logo are registered trademarks of Tyndale House Publishers, Inc. The Tyndale Momentum logo is a trademark of Tyndale House Publishers, Inc. Tyndale Momentum is the nonfiction imprint of Tyndale House Publishers, Inc., Carol Stream, Illinois.

The Coming Apostasy: Exposing the Sabotage of Christianity from Within

Designed by Nicole Grimes

Published in association with the literary agency of William K. Jensen Literary Agency, 119 Bampton Court, Eugene, Oregon, 97404.

For information about special discounts for bulk purchases, please contact Tyndale House Publishers at csresponse@tyndale.com or call 800-323-9400.

ISBN 978-1-4964-1407-6

Printed in the United States of America

23	22	21	20	19	18	17
7	6	5	4	3	2	1

CONTENTS

INTRODUCTION

In NINETEENTH-CENTURY FRANCE, disgruntled workers developed a subversive tactic that involved throwing a shoe into factory machinery, causing it to grind to a halt, ruining all productivity. This act of aggression became known as *sabotage* (from *sabot*, the French word for shoe).[1] A single shoe thrown into the gears could wreak untold havoc on a well-oiled machine.

Today, we are witnessing the relentless sabotage of Christianity and the church from within. Subtle saboteurs are tossing one theological shoe after another into the machine, causing spiritual bewilderment and breakdowns.

Satan has always worked to sabotage the work of God through human false teachers. And although Satan has many shoes and strategies, his two main areas of sabotage are against the *written* Word of God (the Scriptures) and the *living* Word of God (the Savior, Jesus).[2] The devil's first recorded words in the Bible are spoken to Eve in the Garden of Eden, and they drip with doubt and denial: "Indeed, has

God said . . . ?"[3] Since that time, the hiss of the serpent has echoed down through the ages, from generation to generation, as he questions, undermines, and sabotages the Bible. As David Jeremiah says,

> [Satan] isn't just given to one approach. If he can't take the Word of God away from us by undermining its authority, he will take us away from the Word of God by giving us another basis of authority. Satan has developed just such a substitute, and it seems to have a great attraction for many people.
>
> It's called *experience*.
>
> People become so wrapped up in their spiritual experience that they no longer look to the Word of God for their authority. Their experience becomes the determining force in their lives.[4]

Dr. Jeremiah closes with this powerful observation:

> Two groups, then, are vying for our minds—but with the same end in view. [Liberal scholars] would take the Bible away from us, and those who hold to the experiential view would take us away from the Bible.[5]

We could not agree more. Sound doctrine is under siege. The Bible is being either reduced, outright rejected, or replaced by how people feel about whatever moral or theological topic is under consideration.

However, nothing we see should surprise us. The Bible predicted that this day would come. Scripture tells us that the tide of apostasy will crest as the end draws near. This portent of the end is referred to in 2 Thessalonians 2:3 as the falling away or the final great apostasy. That season may be arriving very soon. In light of this sobering reality, our main goal in this book is to unmask the current sabotage aimed at the authority and sufficiency of the Bible and targeting the exclusivity of Jesus as the only way to God. We also want to arm you with the truth, heighten your discernment, and recalibrate your thinking and living in accordance with the plumb line of God's truth. These are serious issues for the church and for every believer. A great deal is at stake.

May the Lord be pleased to use this book in the life of every reader as He has graciously used it already in the lives of its authors.

CHAPTER 1

GOD AND GHOST SHIPS

Some have . . . suffered shipwreck in regard to their faith.

1 TIMOTHY 1:19

CAPTAIN DAVID MOREHOUSE was accustomed to the choppy waters of the North Atlantic, but he wasn't prepared for what caught his eye this winter's day. Sailing some four hundred miles east of the Azores Islands, Morehouse encountered a disturbing sight. It was a ship, which in itself is not unusual to spot on the open sea. What was odd was that this particular two-masted brig seemed to be in great distress. Its canvas sails tattered by a relentless wind, the ship drifted aimlessly in open water. From his vantage point aboard the *Dei Gratia*, Captain Morehouse was unable to see anyone on deck of the wayward vessel. And so, after calling out and receiving no reply, the British captain gave orders to come alongside the mystery ship. He sent a boarding party to inspect the ship, but his first mate and two crew members failed to find a single soul aboard.

Instead, what they discovered was a full cargo containing 1,701 barrels of crude alcohol, along with a six-month supply of food and water. What was missing was the ship's only lifeboat. Gone, too, were its captain, Benjamin S. Briggs, his wife, Sarah, and their two-year-old daughter, Sophia, along with eight crew members. However, they found closets of clothes left behind, suggesting a sudden departure. During the one-hour inspection, the *Dei Gratia*'s boarding crew also observed a disassembled pump and three and a half feet of water sloshing around in the hull. But aside from these curiosities, the 108-foot-long vessel appeared to be seaworthy.

The creaking ship discovered by Captain Morehouse on December 5, 1872, turned out to be the *Mary Celeste*. Records later showed the ship had set sail on November 7 from New York headed for Genoa, Italy. But something happened along the way, and the *Mary Celeste* was now long overdue. And those now aboard the *Dei Gratia*, whose Latin name means "by the Grace of God," could only hope and pray that same grace would watch over the lost ship's passengers and crew.

The tragic tale of the *Mary Celeste* has become one of the most puzzling mysteries in maritime history. Many theories have been offered to make sense of this perplexing story and what happened—everything from pirates to storms and high seas, even sea monsters. Experts still scratch their heads as to why Captain Briggs would give orders to abandon a ship that showed no signs of imminent danger.

But nearly 150 years past that cold December day, and after speculation in articles, books, poems, and even movies, we are today no closer to knowing what led to the *Mary Celeste*'s fate than Morehouse was. In the absence of captain or crew, the ship had drifted off course in the open sea for some two weeks before being discovered. Instead of reaching its intended destination, the *Mary Celeste* has gained the enduring infamy of being history's quintessential ghost ship.

OUR CURRENT CONDITION

Unless you've spent the past few years cast away on a deserted island, you've no doubt come to the conclusion that ours is a planet in peril. We are a culture in chaos, a human race caught in the epicenter of a global storm. Like the *Mary Celeste*, we are adrift as a planet, lost in a turbulent sea of confusion and uncertainty. And it's no longer just the experts who recognize the imminent crises threatening our world. According to a nationwide poll, 41 percent of adults believe we are living in the "end times."[1] An acute awareness of our world's troubles has finally filtered down to the average person. And the reigning consensus is that planet earth is showing all the signs of rapidly approaching disaster on multiple levels.

In other words, we're in deep, choppy waters here.

This moment in time is a markedly different one than our

parents' or grandparents' generation knew. Though previous generations may have witnessed world war, economic recession, and political upheavals, this present dark hour carries a distinctly apocalyptic cargo. Upon first glance, the happenings in recent history may more closely resemble a bad dream or a sci-fi movie scenario. Despite some who naively imagine things getting better, an honest, open-eyed appraisal of humanity's situation reveals much more dystopia than utopia. This is reality, not some hopeful, future fantasy. Further, it's *your* reality. The world in which you live is becoming increasingly volatile, rising and falling like a ship's bow in a furious tempest, wildly tossed about. Instability, unrest, and uncertainty are constants in this contemporary global drama. The world is changing—and not for the better.

Of course, it's human to question and to wonder whether history's hurricane is about to make landfall. Having saturated ourselves in sin, we have to wonder, *Is Revelation finally setting sail toward our shores?*

Scan culture's horizon, and what do we see? Rage-filled citizens rioting in the streets, looting local businesses due to perceived injustice in their community. Immigrants and refugees embroiled in an unprecedented international crisis, the consequences of which are as yet unknown. Mass shootings, combined with an ongoing epidemic of violence and homicide, have almost anesthetized us to murder.[2] And the body count among the unborn continues to rise, nearing 1.5 billion butchered worldwide in the name of "reproductive rights."[3]

The ancient Canaanites got nothing on us.

But that's not all. Keep looking around, and you'll see state and federal authorities, along with Supreme Court justices, passing laws and declaring edicts sanctioning, legalizing, endorsing, promoting, and even wholeheartedly celebrating homosexual activity and same-sex marriage. Men who self-identify as women are allowed to use women's restrooms, exposing young girls to potential trauma, abuse, and attack. Our society's moral conscience has dulled to the point where we now proudly call evil "good" and good "evil." This sad commentary on our nation tragically parallels an earlier time in Israel's history when "everyone did what was right in his own eyes."[4] Today, there's even a proposal within some psychiatric circles to destigmatize sexual offenses such as pedophilia, instead referring to people who commit these offenses as "minor-attracted persons."[5] In our contemporary moral climate, just about anything goes—except, of course, biblical morality. Our culture's collective decadence is eclipsed only by the individual depravity of those who define it. It's a critical breach in humanity's hull, letting in a flood of lunacy disguised as "enlightenment" and "progressive thought." And the water keeps pouring in.

Political correctness has become one of our new idols, and one that demands we pay regular veneration and worship. It dare not be ignored or angered lest we feel its wrath. To merely disagree, for example, with trendy, "richer" views of morality is to be charged with hate speech or bigotry. Historical Judeo-Christian values are systematically being sandblasted from the walls of conscience with pagan, Mardi Gras morals chiseled in their place. To suggest there is still an absolute, objective morality regarding issues such as sexuality or marriage is to be instantly judged, cast into the public court of shame and ridicule, and summarily stoned to death by popular opinion and social media. As a result of this and other glaring evidences of moral decay, many believe we are witnessing in real time the systematic collapse of Western civilization. It's almost as if it were all part of a larger, sinister plan and strategy.

Yes, something is very wrong with *humanity*, something as a race we collectively refuse to acknowledge. In truth, the root causes of our evil obsessions go much deeper than social, psychological, or even moral causes. What lies under the surface of our universal insanity is a spiritual problem, a deadly virus, birthed in our first parents and passed down from generation to generation.

But keep looking, now internationally, and we see that global economic stability has never been so volatile, with multiple nations teetering toward default and financial collapse. According to the World Economic Forum, earth's economy is currently vulnerable on a number of fronts and more than ever at risk to suffer "global shocks." These economic tremors do not respect national borders and can potentially shake whole financial systems and societies to their foundations.[6] Like at no other time in recorded history, the international community has become linked together. What happens financially in one nation often dramatically impacts another, with one country's economic crisis sending concentric ripple effects to ten others, or more. This has led to an unprecedented interdependence in an ever-emerging one-world financial market.

In its Global Risks 2014 Report, the World Economic Forum states, "A fiscal crisis in any major economy could easily have cascading global impacts."[7] Put simply, this worldwide economic house of cards could collapse at any time, an unfolding scenario which seamlessly syncs with Revelation's portrayal of future economic disaster.[8]

Look around, and you'll see that our world is also facing a number of humanitarian crises, one of which is the more than 780 million hungry people in the world today.[9] Though the vast majority of these are from developing countries, they nevertheless represent one out of every eight people on the planet. Imagine the scale of impact when global famine eventually hits the world, as forecast in Revelation. Chances of thriving, both in third-world and developed countries, will rapidly go from unlikely to virtually impossible. Additionally, human trafficking, sex trafficking, and sex slavery together globally form a $32 billion industry involving some 21 million victims worldwide.[10]

What on earth have we become?

From a geopolitical perspective, the Middle East remains a delicate minefield, easily set off by a single misstep. Add to this ticking time bomb Iran's stealthy efforts to develop nuclear weapons capabilities. Iran's stated desire is to remove the Jewish nation as the cancerous "tumor" in the body of the Islamic world, wiping Israel from the face of the earth.[11] Meanwhile, Israel has its own problems as ongoing conflict with Syrian-based Hamas threatens to erupt like a powder keg at any given moment. Recurring missile strikes from both sides are now a regular part of life in the Middle East.

According to Bible prophecy, Russia is poised to be an end-times player and continues to reinforce its reputation as a world bully, having previously established its presence on Israel's border. Drunk on its own power, Russia's next move remains unknown, but this nation could very well be positioning itself for the apocalyptic war Ezekiel predicted.[12]

But there's more.

The Islamic State in Iraq and Syria (ISIS) is the latest unwelcome arrival on the world terrorist scene. Even so, it has managed to have a massive, devastating impact in a relatively short span of time. Begun as a splinter group from al-Qaeda, this barbaric death cult has become well known for military campaigns, invasions, brutal torture, and public executions, including crucifixion. It is apocalyptic Islam on steroids, a brand of jihadist ideology that believes the coming of their Mahdi (messiah) can be hastened as the world is engulfed in chaos and carnage.[13] Ironically, their favorite method of execution is beheading. Reviving an ancient form of bloody barbarism, ISIS has branded itself as a group of modern-day human butchers. Beheadings have now happened right here in the United States, even in rural communities.[14] And these wicked warriors do not discriminate, as they brutally slaughter hundreds of women and small children. The masked monsters of ISIS also produce their own "snuff videos," featuring selected beheadings and executions, posting them online in an attempt to bolster their cause and terrorize peace-loving people worldwide.

This growing terrorist body is well financed and organized. Its short-term goal is to create a "caliphate" (Islamic State) in Syria and Iraq. Forcing over a million Iraqis from their homes, many of them Christians, ISIS has also taken control of oil fields and seized cities in that region. But their gruesome aspirations are not confined to the Middle East. A US Army Intelligence bulletin has warned of potential attacks in America by ISIS supporters and sympathizers targeting US military personnel and their families, threatening to "show up [at their homes] and slaughter them."[15]

Of course, the terrorist roots of this radicalism can be traced back to a several-thousand-year-old hatred of Jews. Now, like a deadly virus, this evil enmity has mutated, branching out with the goal of destroying other equally despised infidels (Christians, friends of Israel, or anyone unwilling to submit to the oppressive religious demands of these sadistic serial murderers).

As if this weren't enough, on American soil, lone-wolf terrorist attacks (sometimes erroneously labeled "workplace violence") have burst the bubble of our assumed protective insulation from this threat. A new tentacle of terrorism has developed as individuals now self-radicalize with bloody vendettas targeting non-Muslims. Unfortunately, there is no guaranteed and effective preventative measure against such rampages.

Negotiation has proved impossible with an ideology whose adherents believe they've been given a "holy mandate" to subjugate or kill outsiders. They do not debate, argue, barter, or waver in fulfilling their mission but are wholly committed to their unholy cause. And there is every indication this brand of terrorism will continue gaining momentum as sleeper cells infiltrate free societies in order to conquer and destroy them. Who would have ever dreamed words like *jihad* and *terrorism* would earn permanent places in our national vocabulary? The imminent threat of another terrorist attack, whether on a local or large scale, is not a matter of *if* but rather *when*, as our military and intelligence leaders believe these jihadists are already on American soil.[16] We do know there are currently some thirty-five Islamic terrorist training camps scattered all across America.[17] These Muslim extremists have also pledged to one day "raise the flag of Allah in the White House."[18]

We have officially passed through the looking glass and into another reality altogether. And there is every indication our world is drifting toward destruction.

But this is what happens when mutiny ensues and humanity defiantly casts God overboard. These are the consequences to resisting and rejecting Him, ripple effects from refusing to acknowledge the Creator's existence and regal right to rule His own creation. God turns us over to ourselves. Billions of people, bound by an enslaving depravity.

However, if our eyes are fixed only on humanity and world events, we could easily be overcome with fear and uncertainty, and often this fear leads to unhealthy isolation and reclusiveness as we withdraw from engaging culture and being Christ's witnesses in the world. Weathering this current sin-storm, Christ's disciples can also default to self-reliance instead of dependence on our Lord, as what's wrong with our world can have a debilitating effect on our faith in God. Looking at the chaos surrounding us, we may even wonder if He is still at the helm. Is God really guiding history? Is He still in charge? Or has He abandoned us altogether?

Were it not for the reality of a sovereign God who superintends both history and humanity, we would surely despair. Thankfully, Scripture assures us the God of heaven is still in control. The real question is, Do we believe that? Daniel 4:35 proclaims, "All the inhabitants of the earth are accounted as nothing, but He does according to His will in the host of heaven and among the inhabitants of earth; and no one can ward off His hand or say to Him, 'What have You done?'"

In light of the darkness around us, the prophet Isaiah delivers much-needed perspective in Isaiah 40:6-31. Open your Bible and read it for yourself, allowing his words to marinate in your mind.

MEANWHILE, AT HOME ...

All across the world, abandoned ships rust on shores and beaches. Some are half sunken while others lie fully submerged under oceans and lakes. These are vessels that suffered shipwreck due to neglect, abandonment, or mutiny. Some were left to drift, sailing aimlessly at the unpredictable whim of the wind and the waves. Many met their fate at the hands of pirates. Forcibly boarding unsuspecting ships, these sea terrorists seized cargo, killing passengers and crew before either scuttling the vessel or leaving it to the ocean's mercy. Still other ships found themselves wandering upon the waters or resting on the ocean floor because of war, storms, fire, disease, a damaged rudder, or running out of fuel or food. Bad winds or no winds easily contribute to the demise of once-worthy ships. Even so, the common denominator for these ghost ships is that they are all *lost*, adrift in the ocean's vast expanse, without help or hope, and with no helmsman to guide them toward safe harbor.

Sadly, what is true of ships can also be true of people. The same perilous danger that threatens seagoing vessels also endangers those who call themselves Christians. It's why the apostle Paul admonished the Corinthians, "Test yourselves to see if you are in the faith; examine yourselves! Or do you not recognize this about yourselves, that Jesus Christ is in you—unless indeed you fail the test?"[19]

Peter, writing to the scattered believers living in a decadent society under the rule of a pagan government, urged, "Therefore, brethren, be all the more diligent to make certain about His calling and choosing you; for as long as you practice these things, you will never stumble; for in this way the entrance into the eternal kingdom of our Lord and Savior Jesus Christ will be abundantly supplied to you."[20]

In a world racing toward Revelation, Jesus' church today finds herself sailing through turbulent waters of her own. She's perilously taking on water while some of her more naive passengers seem perfectly content, satisfying themselves at the weekly Sunday buffet. Mirroring the churches Christ chastised in Revelation 2–3, the collective state of Christendom today faces an internal threat far more deadly than a terrorist attack. As we will discover, the bride of Christ is not exactly "shipshape." In places, she has suffered a hull breach, lost her rudder, failed to catch wind, and gone adrift from the course God has charted for her.

What lies dead ahead is the hidden reef of apostasy, and no one understood this more than Paul, as the much-traveled apostle suffered literal shipwreck himself three times![21] Using this as a powerful metaphor, he puts on display examples of *spiritual* shipwreck, even calling out individuals by name:

> This command I entrust to you, Timothy, my son, in accordance with the prophecies previously made concerning you, that by them you fight the good fight, keeping faith and a good conscience, which some have rejected and *suffered shipwreck* in regard to their faith. Among these are Hymenaeus and Alexander, whom I have handed over to Satan, so that they will be taught not to blaspheme.[22]

There are several important observations and principles we can draw from Paul's words:

1. Losing or abandoning faith is equivalent to apostasy, or suffering "shipwreck."

2. The two men Paul mentions weren't the only ones to abandon the faith.

3. There are tangible, painful consequences to deserting the faith.

Granted, all Christ-followers encounter storms and suffer through occasional seasons of sin. This is a normal part of the challenge and messiness of temptation and sanctification. But there is a vast difference between getting water in your boat and your boat actually sinking, and there is a big distinction between temporarily sailing off course and suffering a fatal shipwreck. The good news is that God has promised to faithfully discipline His children when they, by either active or passive choices, veer off course and straight into sin.[23] At times we may wander, sailing too close to the rocky shore and becoming stuck on those hidden reefs, yet without actually capsizing and permanently going under.

However, for others, there is no rescue from the angry sea or salvage from below. These once-professing believers may have set out on their Christian pilgrimage with good intentions and noble motives. They may have even had a correct course heading, been under great teaching, or participated in a healthy faith community. But as important as those things are, by themselves they are not enough. Thus these self-proclaimed God-followers eventually become spiritual "ghost ships" themselves. It's not an issue of losing their salvation but rather of demonstrating their true identity. They flirted with the idea of being disciples of Jesus at some point in their lives, but their eventual falling away revealed them to be counterfeit Christians. As Jesus bluntly warned, *professing* Him, no matter how confidently, doesn't necessarily mean *possessing* Him.[24] This is why the Holy Spirit inspired John to write, "The one who says, 'I have come to know Him,' and does not keep His commandments, is a liar, and the truth is not in him."[25]

Bottom line: people drift, falter, and sink. So do churches and even whole denominations. Having merely parroted faith in Jesus, they can, and often do, deviate off course. Some succumb to doctrinal error or, like the church at Ephesus, lose the wind in their sails, manifested in the absence of a passionate love for Jesus Christ.[26]

This "falling away from the faith" (known as *apostasy*) can be a nebulous concept, perhaps because it's seldom studied, preached, or understood by a generation of churchgoers who measure their spiritual temperature by how much they "enjoyed" the church service and evaluate their spiritual progress by conformity to rules and religiosity. But our Christian faith goes much deeper than this. Part of maturing as believers means addressing some of the weightier issues of God's Word. As we grow, we discover that, along with all the benefits God offers (His presence; peace; provision; and steadfast, unconditional love), there are also some major concerns He has for His church, specifically, her tendency to drift, both doctrinally and personally. These dangers exist because of the world in which we live, the enemy bent on destroying us, and our own hearts that are so prone to wander.[27] But the closer we get to God's heart, the more our hearts become sensitive and open to the deeper issues God's Word addresses. We begin to want what He wants. That's part of what it means to "seek first [God's] kingdom and His righteousness."[28] At times we may think the really important truths and issues concerning the church are meant only for pastors and leaders. But individual Christians also have a responsibility to preserve the unity and purity of the church.[29] We are *all* meant to understand and "handle the truth." If not, much of Paul's epistles would be irrelevant to the average believer, something we know is not true, as "*all* Scripture is inspired by God and profitable" for us.[30]

As this book will explain, the coming apostasy is a serious sign of the end times and one of Scripture's weightier truths. Understanding it is essential if we are to navigate the waters of today's confusing culture.

THE CAPTAIN OF OUR SALVATION

Apostasy represents an abandonment of faith, and it can happen over time without a person realizing it. In fact, just the opposite may occur, as pride mixed with false doctrine leads to an attitude of superiority, complacency, and self-righteousness. Nevertheless, it's there. Lying just beneath the surface, it is poised to penetrate the very thing keeping us afloat—our faith. Perhaps you've known those who set out seeking safe harbor in Christ only to end up splintered on the jagged rocks of unbelief. Without being moored by the biblical anchor of authentic faith, they drift in an age of unprecedented pseudo-Christian thought. At times they are driven by the winds of progressive theology, postmodern thought, or godless philosophies and values. Perhaps they are emotionally driven by political correctness and even a reimagining of God Himself. In an era of endless information, where self-appointed truth-proclaimers peddle phony faith formulas to innocent, untrained church members, it's no surprise that many become lost in the disorienting fog. This is why every professing believer in Jesus desperately needs a magnetic compass, a map, an anchor, a lighthouse with a clear beacon—an unfailing GPS guiding them every step of the way.

It's also why we need a Captain.

Jesus promised *He* would build His church, "and the gates of Hades will not overpower it."[31] And He has made, and will make, good on that promise. Even so, it's not enough to merely quote verses, claiming immunity from the enemy's attacks. Obviously, because of Christ's efficacious payment for sin, every believer will make it safely to heaven. But that doesn't guarantee a life exempt from sporadic episodes of apathy, self-absorption, moral failure, doctrinal deviance, or even being temporarily misled by false teachers. There is no automatic guarantee of continuous safe spiritual passage. But even in the midst of our messiness and meandering, God is still committed to us—much more committed to us than we are to Him.[32] Yes, Christ will build His church. He has established her and preserved her through both history *and* heresy. And death will not defeat or permanently derail her. But that doesn't mean she isn't vulnerable to rough seas in these last days in which we live. There are clear and present dangers threatening her—threatening *you*, too. There are issues some may consider minor or nonessential but that still cause us to deviate from faith's map. And the longer we continue traveling off course, even if only by a few degrees, the farther from our intended destination we drift.

Pilots who miscalculate flight plans by even one degree could miss their target destinations by hundreds of miles, or worse, run straight into a mountain. Pharmacists who make just one error combining chemicals while filling a prescription could potentially poison their patients.

The same is true for us, which is why we must always strive to stay on target with God and His Word. While Christians may disagree about certain peripheral areas of doctrine, that does not in any way diminish the importance of doctrine itself. And we cannot flippantly dismiss any part of God's Word, because what we believe really does matter.

THE *LORD'S* PRAYER

On Jesus' final night with His disciples, they had dinner together, after which he took them on a walk to a place that was very familiar to them.[33] Located just outside Jerusalem's walls, this garden of olive trees proved to be a favorite gathering spot for Jesus and the Twelve. The word *Gethsemane* comes from two Hebrew words that when combined mean "a place for pressing oil." In ancient culture, heavy slabs of stone were used to crush olives until all the oil had been extracted. The oil was then poured into clay jars for household use. Jesus was well aware of this common practice. He also knew what that word prefigured for Him. Arriving in the garden that night, Christ experienced a sense of dread as He contemplated being crushed by the Father's fierce wrath due to our sin. And so, securing a solitary spot, Jesus fell on His face, pouring out His heart to the Father in prayer.

In that most intimate and passionate prayer, the Son of God explicitly asks the Father *not* to take His followers out of the world but rather to "keep them from the evil one." The reason for this, He says, is that His disciples do not belong to the domain of this world—or of its god.[34] But exactly how would Christ's current and future disciples remain well insulated from Satan's deceptive and destructive influence? The answer is found in the very next verse. They need only for the Father to "sanctify them in the truth," Jesus prays. He then affirms, "Your word is truth."[35]

The life-changing, lasting influence of God's Word in our lives is a primary countermeasure to Satan's attacks. As Jesus' followers, we must keep this in mind when confronting the godless world in which we live. But we also must realize there are other threats too, some coming from within the church itself.

The unfortunate reality today is that the world and the church are often indistinguishable. As worldly philosophies and values infiltrate the body of Christ, moral values adjust and new theologies emerge. This creates a fatal breach, allowing other compromising half-truths and deceptive false teachings into the body. And why would this be such a major concern? Why is it such a big deal? Few things made Paul's blood boil more than false teachers deceiving and misleading God's people.[36] More about this later.

The principle we draw from Jesus' prayer is that we are purified and protected by engaging, believing, and living out God's truth. Put simply, when we think *biblically*, we are less likely to drift aimlessly. But failing to seal our minds from unbiblical thinking, beliefs, and doctrine causes us to sail perilously close to catastrophe. By adjusting Scripture to fit our own thinking (instead of vice versa), we stray from God's heart and mind. And we miss His best for us.

We've written this book for several important reasons: (1) to help you understand what apostasy is; (2) to help you understand that it's surging all around us and is a serious sign of the end times; (3) to guard you from spiritual shipwreck and the danger of sinking; and (4) to help you understand the truth so that you stay on course as you await Christ's return.

Many people today pray for a great revival, and though it may happen, no such revival is prophesied. On the contrary, according to Scripture, a great apostasy is coming.

But how close are we?

CHAPTER 2

THE FIFTH COLUMN

IN 1939, THE SPANISH CIVIL WAR was coming to an end, and General Mola prepared his attack on Madrid. He had four columns of troops ready to take the city, and someone asked Mola which of these would be the first to attack. "The fifth," was his world-famous answer.

General Mola's most important line of attack was not the military outside the city; it was rebel sympathizers inside the city. They went about unnoticed but were already preparing for his advance. The term *fifth column* has come to mean those who sympathize with an attacker and aid the attacker from the inside.[1]

The fifth column within Christianity is apostasy. Let's face it: the word *apostasy* is ugly and harsh—and misunderstood.

Yet the subject is hardly foreign to the Bible. We would all love to talk about positive things and leave the negative to others, but apostasy is an important issue in the New Testament. From its earliest days, the church has faced the advance of apostasy. Many of the New Testament letters were written to confront various forms of false teaching within the churches. Although apostasy is nothing new for the church, in recent times the surge is palpable. As A.W. Tozer wrote, "Christians now chatter learnedly about things simple believers have always taken for granted. They are on the defensive, trying to prove things that a previous generation never doubted."[2] Think of how much more true that statement is today.

TWO WARS

The world today is witnessing two great wars in progress—two wars waged on two fronts. One front is in the East, where radical Islamists are prosecuting a brutal, bloody, barbaric war to establish a caliphate. They want to raise up one religion to dominate the world. The specter of radical Islam casts its ominous shadow across the globe. The other front is in the West. The war in the West is a philosophical war—an attempt to remove one religion, Christianity, from any influence. The war in the East is to establish a religion. The war in the West is to eradicate a religion.

These two wars are closely related. The diminishing role of Christianity in the public square has left the West unable or at least unwilling to stand up against pure evil in the form of ISIS and other militant jihadists. Paralysis and powerlessness are increasingly the response of the West to unmitigated evil. Secularism and humanism have dulled the ability to discern evil, even its most blatant manifestations, and to act against it aggressively.

Christianity is being eviscerated from within and without. From the outside, atheists, secularists, and humanists unload a relentless barrage against the faith. And on the inside, theological liberals and all sorts of false teachers diminish and even deny essential Christian doctrine and morality. This is apostasy, and it's eating away like a cancer at the heart of biblical Christianity.

THE GREAT FALLING AWAY

Before we go any further, let's remind ourselves of the meaning of *apostasy*. Apostasy in general is defection or departure from the tenets of some religious community. The Greek word *apostasia* means "rebellion" or "abandonment." Christian apostasy in its broadest terms is defection or departure from the truth of Scripture. Andy Woods describes it this way:

> The English word apostasy is derived from two
> Greek words. The first word is the preposition *apo*,
> which means "away from." The second word is the
> verb *histēmi*, which means, "to stand." Thus, apostasy
> means, "to stand away from." Apostasy refers to a
> departure from known or previously embraced truth.
> The subject of apostasy has little to do with the

condition of the unsaved world, which has always rejected divine truth and therefore has nothing from which to depart. Rather, apostasy pertains to the spiritual temperature within God's church.[3]

Apostates are those who profess faith but rebel or fall away from it. They never possessed Christ and eternal life but simply professed faith.[4] Apostates are consistently characterized by two things in the New Testament: false doctrine and ungodly living. Apostates believe wrong and behave wrong. "They profess to know God, but by their deeds they deny Him."[5] Apostates are the fifth column within the visible church.

Some apostates deny the faith and leave the church. Others deny the faith and stay within the church. While both are harmful, those who remain and persist in eroding the foundation of the church of Jesus Christ are worse. We live in days of rampant, surging, encroaching apostasy. The fifth column is firmly entrenched in almost all the major denominations in America today and has overrun most theological seminaries in what is nothing short of a landslide. Every aspect of Christianity is under sustained attack. Doctrinal underpinnings are being challenged and jettisoned at an accelerated pace. We are witnessing a startling departure from the truth on the part of individuals, churches, and even entire denominations. Sound doctrine is under siege.

The rise of modern technology, which has aided the spread of the gospel and the reach of sound biblical teaching, has also given voice to an endless barrage of teaching from those who regularly undercut the truth of Scripture. The blogosphere is fertile ground for shallow, shady, and even satanic teaching that clouds and confuses many believers and provides ammunition for apostates. Gaining a following is easier than ever.

Of course, the church has always been plagued by apostasy but nothing like what we see today. Recently, for example, a professor at a respected Christian college said that Islam and Christianity worship the same God. Of course, this statement is incorrect on its face because the God of Christianity is a triune God (one God in three persons—Father, Son, and Holy Spirit) while Islam denies the deity of Christ. Christianity teaches that Jesus is the only way to God, so if you deny Him, you cannot come to God. The college moved to fire the professor who said God and Allah are the same, which we applaud, but her statement (and the conversation it generated) unveils a growing sentiment that clear biblical doctrine is cloudy, confused, and even contradicted.

Apostasy has been around since the beginning of the church. But could the surge of apostasy over the last few decades be another sign that the coming of the Lord is near? Is the rise of apostasy a harbinger of the end times? Could the church today be on the threshold of that terrible dark period predicted at the end of the age?

TIMES OF THE SIGNS

The key to putting together a puzzle is the picture on top of the box. All the pieces, when fitted together, will look like this picture. The Bible lays out a detailed picture of the end-times template or scenario, which serves as the picture on top of the box. Our world today is looking more and more all the time like that picture. Here are a few of the key puzzle pieces we see fitting into place.

Regathering of the Jewish People

Many of the end-times prophecies of Scripture hinge in one way or another on the presence of the Jewish people in their ancient homeland. Against all odds, the Jewish people, after almost two thousand years of dispersion, are coming back to their land. Almost 40 percent of the Jewish people have returned, and as Scripture predicts, they are under constant attack or the imminent threat of attack. The modern state of Israel has been rightly called the supersign of the end times.

Rise of Globalism

Globalism is another discernible sign of the times. Scripture predicts in many places that the world in the end times will be under the rule of one man.[6] The world will come full circle in the end times. Just as Nimrod ruled the world in the days after the Flood, before people were scattered across the face of the earth, Satan will bring the world back together again under the rule of one man he controls.[7] Globalism, accelerated by technology and an international economy, strikingly foreshadows what Scripture presents.

Ratification of a Peace Treaty

According to Scripture, the end times will begin with a peace treaty between the final world ruler (the Antichrist) and the nation of Israel.[8] Other biblical references point toward a brief time of global peace as the end times begin.[9] The global cry today for peace in troubled times points toward where things are headed. The world is anxious to find someone who can bring security and peace to our ravaged planet.

Rumors of Wars in the Middle East

World focus on the Middle East is another sign of the times. The staging ground for many of the events of the end of the age is in this region. The spotlight of the world is on the ravaged Middle East today, just as we should expect if the coming of the Lord is near.

The nations listed in Ezekiel 38:1-7 (including Russia, Iran, and Libya) are all existing nations with the will and desire to attack Israel, just as Ezekiel prophesied over 2,500 years ago.

Rebellion of Apostasy

Many other significant signs could be mentioned. Yet one sign of the end times that is often ignored or overlooked is the rise of apostasy, or the final great falling away. Andy Woods writes, "Apostasy is another sign, often taking place right under our noses, which we fail to recognize as a sign of the end. Apostasy is the specific scriptural sign given indicating that the church is nearing the completion of her earthly mission."[10] The New Testament says that the final great apostasy is coming. To understand this future event, we have to turn to 2 Thessalonians 2.

APOSTASY AND THE APOCALYPSE

The apostle Paul's letters to the Thessalonians were written during his second missionary journey during his stay in Corinth.[11] While these epistles address many important topics, their outstanding feature is a focus on the future. They are often called the "eschatological epistles" since the coming of the Lord is mentioned in every chapter.

Second Thessalonians 2 is one of the great prophetic chapters of Scripture. No other chapter in the entire Bible covers the same prophetic ground. To understand this chapter and its content, we have to know a little background. Sometime not long after Paul wrote his first letter to the Thessalonians, teachers arose in the church who were espousing false doctrine. The nature of this particular false teaching was that the Day of the Lord had come and the church was already in the Great Tribulation. The Tribulation or Day of the Lord is the final time of global judgment that precedes the second coming of Christ. Apparently, this false teaching erupted in several forms, one of which was a forged, spurious letter that claimed to be from the apostle Paul. Before straightening this problem out, Paul frames the issue:

> Now concerning the coming of our Lord Jesus
> Christ and our being gathered together to him, we
> ask you, brothers, not to be quickly shaken in mind
> or alarmed, either by a spirit or a spoken word, or
> a letter seeming to be from us, to the effect that the
> day of the Lord has come.[12]

While it may seem strange to us that the new believers at Thessalonica would entertain the teaching that the end-times Day of the Lord had arrived, we have to remember that they were enduring serious persecution (as reflected in 2 Thessalonians 1). Their current persecution made them susceptible to the notion that the Day of the Lord had already arrived. It all made sense in light of their circumstances. Nevertheless, the reality of being in the Day of the Lord raised a major issue. Paul, in his first letter to them (1 Thessalonians), promised them deliverance from the future time of tribulation by means of their catching away or Rapture to heaven.[13] If what they were now being told was true, it would mean either that Paul's previous teaching about their deliverance was wrong or that Paul had been correct, and they had been left behind.[14] Neither of these prospects was appealing, and they were seriously shaken "with the impact of a major earthquake, and they were continuing to feel the disturbing aftershocks of that report."[15]

The question facing the Thessalonians is whether their present sufferings indicate they had already entered the tribulation period. Paul's answer to this question is an emphatic no.

He tells the Thessalonians they are not in the Day of the Lord. In order to drive his answer home, he points to two things that must transpire before that day can come, which hadn't happened yet: "Let no one deceive you in any way. For that day will not come, unless the rebellion comes first, and the man of lawlessness is revealed, the son of destruction."[16] Two things must happen before the end times can begin: an event must occur (the rebellion) and a person must appear (the rebel).

Paul's point is clear: because neither of these events had taken place, the Day of the Lord could not have come. But it will come someday.

THE APPROACHING APOSTASY

The first event that must come before the final Day of the Lord is the apostasy, or the rebellion. Paul is saying that the final Day of the Lord cannot come until there is a widespread departure from the true faith. Some take the departure here to be a physical departure, or the Rapture of the church to heaven. While that view has some merit, most expositors believe that this refers to a theological departure or rebellion.[17]

The definite article appears before the word "apostasy" signaling that this is not just any departure from the faith but one that is unique and that the readers apparently knew about. It is *the* apostasy. This final apostasy will entail a large-scale, widespread falling away on the part of those who profess to know God. Some scholars see the apostasy in 2 Thessalonians 2:3 in broader terms, referring to a "world-wide rebellion against authority at the end of the age"—that is, a general uprising against God.[18] While that will certainly occur, in the context of 2 Thessalonians 2:1-3, the apostasy seems to describe a departure on the part of those who profess to know God. John Calvin notes,

> Paul therefore uses the term rebellion or 'apostasy' to mean a treacherous departure from God, not on the part of one person or a few individuals, but such as would spread far among a wide circle of people. Now, nobody can be called an apostate but he who had previously professed to follow Christ and the Gospel. Paul, therefore, is predicting a general rebellion in the visible church.[19]

Referring to 2 Thessalonians 2:3, G. K. Beale says, "The apostasy will not occur primarily in the non-Christian world but rather within the covenant community."[20] Christendom is headed for a great falling away. At the time 2 Thessalonians was written, there were, no doubt, some errors in the church, but there was no widespread apostasy within Christianity in the ordinary sense of the term. The churches were still true to the Lord. Paul is declaring that the Day of the Lord cannot come until there is first a pervasive, global departure from the faith. The Scriptures speak often of this coming apostasy (see the next section, "From Bad to Worse").

In the twenty-first century the situation is entirely different than it was for the Thessalonian church. Today there is certainly widespread apostasy. The sad fact is that there are many who are not preaching the true gospel and moreover are denying the central doctrines of our Christian faith. Many are teaching that Christ is only a man, that He was not born of a virgin, that He was not sinless, that He did not rise from the dead, that salvation is not through His atoning sacrifice, that people can get to heaven other than through Jesus, and that He is not coming again. They deny that the Scriptures are the inerrant, infallible Word of God and decide what parts of the Bible are important and which parts are optional or even outdated. They reject the biblical standards for holy living and accept practices such as homosexual activity, even among church leaders. To a certain degree, apostasy is already here and swelling in strength and intensity.

The second event that must occur before the final Tribulation can begin is the revelation or unveiling of the "man of sin." This man of sin is none other than the final Antichrist. "Man of sin" is one of his many aliases recorded in Scripture. The verses that follow describe the outrageous nature of his sin: "[He] opposes and exalts himself against every so-called god or object of worship, so that he takes his seat in the temple of God, proclaiming himself to be God."[21] The Antichrist's outrageous self-deification will be the final step downward in man's rebellion against the true God.

The relationship between the apostasy and the Antichrist is clear. The final great falling away will prepare the world for the reception of the final Antichrist. John Stott summarizes this well:

> What he does is to clarify the order of future events. *The day of the Lord* (2b) cannot be here already, he says, because *that day will not come* until two other things have happened. A certain event must take place, and a certain person must appear. The event he calls *the rebellion* (*apotasia*, "the Great Revolt" JB; "the final rebellion against God" REB) and the person *the man of lawlessness*, the rebel. Although Paul does not call him the "Antichrist," this is evidently who he is. John writes of the expectation of his coming.[22]

Charles Ryrie adds, "It is as though the infidelity of those who profess to be religious will prepare the way and perhaps even furnish the occasion for the final display of revolting against God in the person of the Man of Sin. But the Day of the Lord will not be present until this great apostasy sweeps the earth."[23] As those who profess to know the truth turn wholesale from it, they will embrace the ultimate lie—worshiping a man as God.

FROM BAD TO WORSE

A handful of New Testament passages tell us that apostasy will be one of the defining characteristics of the last days.

Each of the following passages provides important insight into the nature of apostasy in the last days.

1 Timothy 4:1-3

First Timothy 4:1 states, "The Spirit explicitly says that in later times some will fall away from the faith, paying attention to deceitful spirits and doctrines of demons."

The time frame of when this apostasy will occur is defined as "later times." The word "later" or "latter" indicates that these times were still future when Paul wrote this epistle. The word used here for "times" is the Greek word *kairois*. It refers to seasons or shorter segments of time. It is plural to indicate that there will be more than one of them—that is, these times of apostasy will recur intermittently throughout the church age.[24]

2 Timothy 3:1-13

This extended passage contains some of the final words of the apostle Paul—words of warning. In these verses, Paul catalogs nineteen characteristics that will prevail during various seasons throughout the last days of the church. These conditions will worsen as the church age progresses. We will look at this passage in more detail in chapter 6.

2 Peter 2:1-22; 3:3-6

In 2 Peter 2:1-22, the apostle writes a lengthy diatribe against apostates that he predicts will come into the church to deceive God's people and deny and disobey the truth.

Second Peter 2:1-2 says, "False prophets also arose among the people, just as there will also be false teachers among you, who will secretly introduce destructive heresies, even denying the Master who bought them, bringing swift destruction upon themselves. Many will follow their sensuality, and because of them the way of the truth will be maligned."

In 2 Peter 3:3-4, Peter continues, "Know this first of all, that in the last days mockers will come with their mocking, following after their own lusts, and saying, 'Where is the promise of His coming?'" Peter says apostates will even deny the second coming of Christ.

Jude 1:1-25

Jude, a half-brother of Jesus, writes his entire brief epistle as a warning that the apostates Peter had warned about a few years earlier have already arrived, worming their way into the church. I (Mark) have always found it interesting that the little epistle of Jude, which is the only book in the Bible devoted exclusively to apostasy, is right before the book of Revelation. In many ways, Jude serves as the vestibule or foyer for the book of Revelation by revealing what the visible, professing church will be like in the days before the events of Revelation unfold.

SIGN OF THE TIMES?

In Scripture, apostasy possesses a "specific eschatological orientation."[25] The apostasy we see swelling today is all headed toward the final, full-blown falling away predicted in 2 Thessalonians 2:3, which Scripture says will break out as the end times begin to unfold. Many today are expecting a great global revival as the end nears. Of course, that's possible, and we hope and pray it will come, but John Phillips gives some helpful biblical perspective:

> The river of apostasy is rising today. The "perilous times" of which Paul wrote are upon us. Soon the river will overflow its banks as all the tributaries of delusion and deception join the mainstream. When it reaches flood level, that river will inundate the earth in the final apostasy, which is the enthronement of the Devil's messiah as this world's god and king. . . . Some think we can look for a worldwide spiritual awakening before the Rapture of the church, but this passage in 2 Thessalonians indicates the opposite; a worldwide departure from the faith can be expected. God might indeed send a revival before He calls home the church, but the Scriptures do not prophesy one.[26]

Deepening apostasy is a sign of the times. Apostasy to some degree has always been within the church, but a future, distinct period of moral darkness and spiritual deception is coming. There is no doubt today that deepening deception and surging apostasy are upon us. What we see in the visible church today is nothing short of shocking. We are witnessing the increase and intensification of apostasy we should expect if the coming of Christ is near. While things could always get worse, we find it difficult to believe that they could get much worse than the theological and moral malaise we have witnessed in the last fifty years, and especially the last decade. We seem to be on the leading edge of the final apostasy, and as the end nears, the battle will intensify.

In case you think we're overreacting or are alone in our assessment of apostasy as a sign of the end times, here are some quotes from well-known, respected pastors and prophecy teachers who share this viewpoint.

John Walvoord, former president of Dallas Theological Seminary, in his book *The Church in Prophecy*, believes what we see today is a sign of the times:

> The increment of evil, the growth of hypocrisy, selfishness, and unbelief within the bounds of professing Christendom are according to Scripture signs of the approaching end of the age. Though there are thousands of faithful congregations and many pious souls still bearing a faithful testimony to Christ in our modern day, it is hardly true that the majority of Christendom is bearing a true testimony. It is the exception rather than the rule for the great fundamentals of the church to ring from the pulpit and for the pew to manifest the transforming grace of God in life and sacrificial devotion. In a word, the

last days of the church on earth are days of apostasy, theologically and morally, days of unbelief, and days that will culminate in divine judgment.[27]

Walvoord concludes, "The Scriptures predict that there will be a growing apostasy or departure from the Lord as the church age progresses, and its increase can be understood as a general indication that the Rapture itself is near."[28]

J. Dwight Pentecost, a noted authority on Bible prophecy, states,

> Abundant evidence on every hand shows that men are departing from the faith. Not only do they doubt the Word; they openly reject it. This phenomenon has never been as prevalent as today. In the period of church history known as the Dark Ages, men were ignorant of the truth; but never was there an age when men openly denied and repudiated the truth. This open, deliberate, willful repudiation of the truth of the Bible is described in Scripture as one of the major characteristics of the last days of the church on earth.[29]

John Harold Ockenga was a leading figure of American evangelicalism in the mid-twentieth century. He pastored Park Street Church in Boston and helped found Fuller Seminary and Gordon-Conwell Theological Seminary. Commenting on apostasy as a sign of the times, he said,

"In this present great apostasy from New Testament Christianity we could see a sign which will warrant us in believing that Christ's coming may not be far away. There has always been some measure of apostasy and at times that apostasy has been great, but not as it has been in the last fifty years."[30]

Donald Grey Barnhouse, the great Presbyterian pastor, said, "Watch for such an apostasy, says Paul; that will be the sign of the day of the Lord. Well, it is possible that we may be seeing the first stages of such apostasy in our day. If ever there was a turning away from the truth, it is in our day. . . . But we're seeing the tip of the iceberg."[31]

John Horsch, writing back in the early part of the twentieth century, said,

> The apostasy that is evident on every hand is an unmistakable sign of the times. It should arouse believing Christendom from its lethargy and listlessness to a realization of conditions as they are. In consequence of the apostasy the church finds itself today face to face with a crisis such as it has never passed through in its history.[32]

These are the last days of apostasy for the church. We are not yet in the final, great falling away that will immediately presage the arrival of the end times, but we are on the vanguard.

In the pages to come we want to get more specific about

some of the areas where apostasy is accelerating and give practical, hopeful encouragement that will help us wake up and stand up and run our leg of the race faithfully, passing the baton intact to the next generation if our Lord doesn't come first.

CHAPTER 3

FAITH OF OUR FATHERS

As for you, speak the things which are fitting for sound doctrine.

TITUS 2:1

WE LIVE IN A WORLD where feelings trump rational thought, where a statement may be considered "true" not because it actually is but simply because it feels right or because someone wants it to be true. Take any biblical truth—whether concerning God's sovereignty, the reality of eternal punishment, or marriage between a man and a woman only—and if it clashes with someone's personal belief or desire for what reality should be, it is simply redefined or dismissed altogether. The prevailing spirit of the age is one where individuals can now craft their own truth-world, one that fits them and their perception of reality.

It is in this sense that humans have essentially crowned themselves little gods. And as fantastical as that may sound, it's how most people practically function. We take truth, doctrine, and moral decisions into our own hands and fall for the deception our first parents embraced in the Garden. Questioning the clearly revealed will and Word of God, Adam and Eve believed that personal fulfillment and happiness lay somewhere outside their loving Father's provision. And so, drifting from His truth and plan, they bit the bait and bought the lie, becoming "like God."[1]

And here we are.

Thousands of years later, we still think we can deviate from God's Word and somehow not die. The intoxicating lure of being in charge of our own lives and of scriptwriting our own reality is often a temptation too pleasurable to resist. But it is only when we acknowledge that there is a God and we're not Him that our minds can clear and we can begin enjoying a satisfying relationship with our Creator. Ours is not a blind faith, and when we believe without reason, we are easily persuaded away from God's truth by a more promising or persuasive argument.

So it brings us to the question: Why do you believe what you believe? The question is not as much about evidence as it is about *impetus*. In other words, what factors motivate you toward acceptance and ownership of a particular belief? When you say you believe a biblical truth, where does that belief come from? Some might say:

- My parents taught it to me.
- It's what my pastor believes.
- I read it in a Christian book.

- A famous Christian said it.
- It just feels right.
- It's what I've always believed.
- It gives me comfort to believe it.
- It makes me happy.
- It seems more inclusive.
- I can't imagine God behaving otherwise.
- I seriously studied it.
- It's in the Bible.

When you look at the sources of our faith and why we choose to embrace a certain doctrine or truth as our own, it becomes clear that only one source is 100 percent reliable. The bottom line of any belief is that if it can't be backed up by Scripture, it's nothing more than wishful thinking, speculation, or theory. So then, how exactly is belief formed? What is it? Does having a conviction really matter anymore? And if so, why?

According to the Bible, biblical belief is more than intellectual agreement. It's more than just a spiritual nodding of the head. Rather, it occurs when both the mind and the will engage God's truth. Volition is involved, as faith is a conscious choice. Belief connects with the spirit. And that belief then informs and influences a person's thinking, focusing the lens through which he or she sees God, life, others, the world, and reality itself. That kind of faith, stemming from Scripture, gives us a discernment that helps us navigate the confusing, contradictory world in which we live.

Some today argue, "What difference does it make what you believe as long as you love God and others? Aren't those the greatest commandments?" Yes, those are the greatest commandments, but if that were the sum total of all God wanted us to know, believe, and do, the sixty-six books of the Bible would be reduced to two verses. There is a greatest commandment, but it in no way diminishes our responsibility to all the others. Besides, who is this God we are commanded to love with all our heart? What do we know about Him? What has He done? What is He like?

It is not possible to effectively love or worship a God about whom we know nothing. Further, the more we know about this great God, the more we are drawn into deeper love for and worship of Him. Therefore, we must encounter truth about Him, otherwise our love has no real object, and we end up once again with a god manufactured in our own minds.

If we truly believe all of the Bible is divinely inspired, then *every word* of it is, as Paul wrote, "useful to teach us what is true and to make us realize what is wrong in our lives. It corrects us when we are wrong and teaches us to do what is right. God uses it to prepare and equip his people to do every good work."[2]

The beauty of this is that it means God intends for us to go beyond merely "savoring the Psalms." He also invites us to dive into Deuteronomy, study 2 Timothy, and read Revelation. It means we care about 2 Chronicles as well as Colossians. How tragic that Christians often treat books of the Bible like outdated clothes in the closet: "I don't like that one anymore.

This one doesn't fit me. It's old, out of season, or no longer in fashion. No one is wearing that style anymore."

But although truth may indeed go "out of style" in society, God and His Word never change. Therefore, those who believe His truth recognize that they will, at times, become unpopular or even hated as their beliefs race toward a head-on collision with culture. According to Jesus, this is part of discipleship and to be expected.[3]

WHY TRUTH MATTERS

Have you noticed how people today are selective about which parts of the Bible they accept as historical, true, relevant, and necessary for life in the twenty-first century? Even in some mainline denominations, many are choosing to go with the "basics of the faith," ignoring, dismissing, or outright denying the rest of God's Word as optional or even, as popular author Rob Bell has suggested, "irrelevant" to today's culture.[4] Sort of like passing over the pickled okra at the salad bar, there is a growing movement among Christianized millennials toward a *figurative* rather than literal understanding of the Bible. Among their discussions is a reimagining of gender, the Genesis creation account, marriage and divorce, the role of women in the church, and homosexuality.[5]

This is definitely not your father's faith. Nor is it Paul's.

But it's a fair question to ask: How much does the *content* of our faith really matter? Is there really only one faith to which we should all subscribe? Or are there just a few core truths, with the rest of it being whatever we want to believe?

One way to address this issue is to remember that truth doesn't exist in a vacuum. We live in a world where there is both good and evil, virtue and vice. There is a God and an actual devil, and there is a sinful nature inside each of us that resists God and rebels against Him. Satan, self, and a planet saturated with sin together create an environment where lies and evil are as plentiful as the air we breathe:

- Lies about God, humanity, happiness, and the afterlife
- Theories of origins birthed in darkened minds and intellects devoid of truth or the willingness to entertain it
- Lies about what and who we are as humans
- Purposeful deceptions about gender, strategically planted in our collective consciousness by the great deceiver himself

Breathing this atmosphere sometimes makes it difficult to distinguish between the truth, half-truths, and full-blown lies. Every day, we walk through a minefield of falsehood. This is why the author of Hebrews wrote that mature believers are those "who because of practice have their senses trained to discern good and evil."[6] Growing in the grace and knowledge of our Lord and Savior is part of what safely maneuvers us through that minefield.[7] Simply put, understanding and believing God's truth enables us to discern the distinction between the truth and Satan's subtle lies.[8]

But that's not all. Sound doctrine does much more for you:

- It nourishes you in the faith.[9]
- It keeps you true to God when, in the last days, people downplay the importance of biblical teaching, even dismissing and denying it.[10]
- It helps you to encourage other believers in the truth and to refute those who blatantly contradict Scripture.[11]

For example, in His encounter with the Samaritan woman, Jesus not only exposes and corrects her flawed theology but He also enlightens her understanding regarding the nature of true worship:

You Samaritans know very little about the one you worship, while we Jews know all about him, for salvation comes through the Jews. But the time is coming—indeed it's here now—when true worshipers will worship the Father in spirit and in truth. The Father is looking for those who will worship him that way. For God is Spirit, so those who worship him must worship in spirit and in truth.[12]

Jesus isn't afraid of offending this woman or hurting her feelings, because He knows that's not what love is or how it operates. Instead, He genuinely cares for her and wants her very best; therefore, He communicates the truth in a way that makes sense to her, even though it may be a bit uncomfortable in spots.

Think about it. God conceived of and created not only the human body but also the mind and the spirit.[13] So it stands to reason that He would know how they best operate, how they connect with Him, and how they bring Him maximum glory. Jesus is teaching here that worshiping in spirit cannot be divorced from the knowledge of the truth. Logically and chronologically, true worship must begin with the revelation of God's truth to our minds. Mindless worship, therefore, is an oxymoron. Being spiritually or emotionally caught up in worship requires some previous knowledge of the One you are worshiping. Otherwise it is nothing more than an imaginative exercise, a fantasy of faith. Authentic worship begins with *knowing* something about God. So knowledge of God (sound teaching) naturally leads to worshiping God, and we should never experience one without the other.

God made us to *know*. He designed our minds to reason, wonder, inquire, explore, and comprehend. As a result, the Christian faith is more than just wishing, hoping, or believing. It involves a level of intellectual confidence in the truth God has revealed, from general revelation (creation and conscience) to special revelation (Christ and Scripture).[14] Therefore, belief based on knowledge about God and His revealed truth is what actually *enables* us to enter into worship and become what Jesus calls a "true worshiper."[15] Otherwise we may worship a false image of God, which is what the Bible calls idolatry. It cheats us out of the full experience of enjoying who He really is![16]

Paul writes,

> Though we walk in the flesh, we do not war according to the flesh, for the weapons of our warfare are not of the flesh, but divinely powerful for the destruction of fortresses. We are destroying speculations and every lofty thing raised up against the knowledge of God, and we are taking every thought captive to the obedience of Christ.[17]

What are these "fortresses" Paul speaks about here? A fortress is a stronghold, a place of strength. Paul identifies them here as "speculations," which are human (or demonically inspired) thoughts, ideas, beliefs, theories, opinions, philosophies, doctrines, and so on—anything that contrasts with the true knowledge of God as found in Scripture. Paul includes "every lofty thing," meaning those ideas or philosophies that are proposed or presented as wise, learned, established, scientific, or superior to the Word.

Paul calls them "fortresses" because they are mental and spiritual strongholds that capture our thinking concerning God, truth, and life. They take our thoughts captive, enslaving them into false patterns of thinking. But the Christian influenced by the Word can rescue those thoughts by exposing the lies for what they really are. Thus we turn the tables on Satan's strategies, taking those thoughts captive to the obedience of Christ.

A few years ago, I (Jeff) wrote a book about the doctrine of the sin nature—what it is, how it operates, and how we can overcome it. Using the metaphor of zombies, I portrayed the sin nature as the "living dead" within that longs to consume us. As a result, I was invited to speak and exhibit my book at an international zombie convention in Seattle. Out of the over seven thousand zombie and horror movie enthusiasts in attendance, several hundred came to hear me speak. Perhaps they were curious what a Christian author could possibly say at a zombie convention.

The moderator of the session (John) was an avowed atheist. And just to mock me and ridicule my faith, he wore a priest's collar during the entire interview. As we both took the stage, he introduced me this way: "Author Jeff Kinley will now tell us more about his zombie book, and also I'm sure a little bit about his imaginary friend . . . *God.*"

Following that introduction, he began firing question after question, attacking both the church and Christianity with an air of superiority and self-righteousness (and with some well-chosen expletives thrown in). Some of what he said about the state of the church I agreed with. But with every "lofty thing" and "speculation" he shot my way, I countered with reasonable truth from Scripture. Finally, frustrated that his antagonistic arguments were getting him nowhere (*and* steadily losing his credibility with the audience), he threw up his hands and asked, "Okay, so enough about the book. Just answer me this. Why would a guy like you ever get into this 'Jesus thing' in the first place?"

I looked at him, amazed, thinking, *Did I hear him correctly? Did he really just ask me to share my Christian testimony with all these people?*

I thanked God for His sovereignty and ability to overrule the futile plans of men. I told my story of coming to faith in Christ and how He still helps me overcome my personal zombie within (sin nature). Afterward many people stayed around to ask questions and purchase books, so I didn't get to say good-bye to John. However, later that afternoon, I paid him a visit at his booth (he was a newspaper journalist turned comic book writer). I offered him a signed copy of my book, and he gratefully accepted. As I turned to leave, he offered an unexpected apology.

"Hey, I'm sorry if I was a little too hard on you up there today."

I smiled and gave him a firm handshake.

We parted as friends.

Fortunately that day my knowledge of Scripture helped me destroy human speculations and philosophies. Had I not been "nourished on the words of faith and of sound doctrine," John and his arguments could have eaten me for lunch . . . like a *zombie*!

Most of the spiritual battles we face don't happen on a stage in front of hundreds of people but out there in the real world—in the classroom, at work, or with neighbors, friends, or even family. Much of the time our battleground is more hidden, taking place in the privacy of our own minds. And I don't always win those skirmishes. Sometimes I know the truth but fail to follow it. Other times I rationalize it for my own selfish benefit.

So knowing Scripture is only half the battle. Like Jesus, when tempted by Satan's deceptions, we have to go beyond merely quoting the truth to *obeying* it.[18]

But with all this talk about knowledge and sound doctrine, you might think, *Wait a minute. Didn't Paul say "knowledge puffs up, but love is really what edifies"?*[19] That's absolutely true. Knowledge, when not accompanied by humility, obedience, love, and worship, can easily birth pride in us. Often when people know something others don't, they feel superior and use that knowledge to put others down while at the same time exalting themselves. This is true of those who reject God's revelation about creation, replacing it with their own theories. Paul says these people became "futile in their speculations, and their *foolish* [literally 'unintelligent' or 'without understanding'] heart was darkened." The result is that "professing to be wise, they became fools."[20]

But Christians can also fall prey to this type of arrogance. When we pursue knowledge for knowledge's sake or when we fail to apply what God's Word reveals to us, we are setting ourselves up to become proud and bloated. That's why we must always receive God's truth with humility, responding with love and worship toward Him. Real knowledge of God is far more than fact gathering. Doctrine isn't simply a systematic collection of truths or storing up "Bible ammunition."

No, the *Word* of God always leads us to the *person* of God. It is never an end unto itself. Truth comes *from* God *to* us in order that we may respond accordingly and live that truth back to God. "For from Him and through Him and to Him are all things. To Him be the glory forever. Amen."[21]

This is the purpose of all knowledge and sound doctrine. It's why Paul writes to the Philippians,

> This is my prayer: that your love may abound more and more in *knowledge* and depth of insight, *so that* you may be able to discern what is best and may be pure and blameless for the day of Christ, filled with the fruit of righteousness that comes through Jesus Christ—to the glory and praise of God.[22]

For the Colossians, he prays,

> For this reason also, since the day we heard of it, we have not ceased to pray for you and to ask that you may be filled [influenced] with the *knowledge* of His will in all spiritual wisdom and understanding, *so that* you will walk in a manner worthy of the Lord, to please Him in all respects, bearing fruit in every good work and *increasing in the knowledge of God*.[23]

Jesus even defined "eternal life" itself as *knowing* the Father: "This is eternal life, that they may know You, the only true God, and Jesus Christ whom You have sent."[24]

Biblical knowledge is meant to be both intellectual *and* experiential.[25] It's a package deal—two sides to the same coin and meant to be enjoyed together. Knowledge without response is like an incomplete sentence or a song without a chorus. Information about God must always lead to an intimacy with Him. It's as much true now as it will one day be in heaven, when our intimacy with God will be exponentially enhanced by a more complete knowledge of Him.[26]

Can you see how growing in your knowledge of God and His Word is essential to becoming mature and complete in your faith?[27]

CHRISTIAN CONTENDERS

So how do we apply this knowledge as it relates to the coming apostasy and the false doctrine currently swirling around us? It's important to note that though the purity of the Christian faith has been preserved and passed down for two thousand years, as history records, it hasn't always been a smooth handoff. There have been seasons and even centuries where the truth taught in the church was altered, modified, and even denied, all in the name of God. It took courageous men of faith like Martin Luther, John Calvin, and Ulrich Zwingli calling the church *out* and *back* to her scriptural roots. And in doing so, they also called her *up*, toward godliness and maturity in Christ. This is the faith we are commanded to defend. In Jude's letter we read, "Beloved, while I was making every effort to write you about our common salvation, I felt the necessity to write to you appealing that you *contend earnestly for the faith* which was once for all handed down to the saints."[28]

"The faith" Jude refers to is the body of truth found in Scripture. This truth is not a fluid, ongoing revelation but rather one that was "once for all" delivered to God's people. This is one reason why we reject so-called visions and supposed visits to heaven claiming new revelation not found in Scripture. The Christian faith has been entrusted to *us*, deposited into our hearts and minds. God is counting on us to "guard what has been entrusted" to us and to "hold on to the pattern of wholesome teaching" we have learned.[29] Paul exhorted Timothy, "Through the power of the Holy Spirit who lives within us, *carefully guard* the precious truth that has been *entrusted* to you."[30]

But exactly why would Jude call us to vigorously contend for the faith? And why would Paul strongly exhort us to guard that faith? Why does Scripture urge us to fight for the truth? Simple: "Certain persons have crept in unnoticed, those who were long beforehand marked out for this condemnation, ungodly persons who turn the grace of our God into licentiousness and deny our only Master and Lord, Jesus Christ."[31]

Plainly put—false teachers. Wolves disguised as sheep. Counterfeits. *Apostates.*

It's not a topic you hear much about in the church today, even though the Bible addresses the subject repeatedly and prophetically. But why not? Why does theology seem so important to Jude and Paul? Why does God take the truth so seriously? Shouldn't we stick to everyday issues, problems, and "practical applications" for our lives?

This is where we need a paradigm shift in the church. According to Jesus and the New Testament writers, theology and doctrine *are* practical matters. And they are definitely not just for preachers, theologians, and "Bible nerds." The Word of God was written for the common person. God wants every one of His children to read and comprehend His Word.

Besides, even the youngest believer knows some theology and doctrine. When you say, "I believe Jesus died on the cross for me to take away my sin," *that's* doctrine and theology.[32] Theology is the study of God, and doctrine simply refers to a system of teaching or a body of belief. Our faith is not primarily a feeling. It is *belief* based on fact. It's more about grounded assurance than personal philosophy. Like other disciplines such as math or science, we can't simply make up facts or imagine things about God and then base our lives on those thoughts. To do so is to make a radical departure from Scripture and the historical beliefs of the early church. Instead, we always must calibrate our thoughts about God to biblical truth, regardless of contemporary or popular thinking, faith fads, or theological trends. That's because *true* knowledge begins with God.[33]

You wouldn't adamantly assert that $2 + 2 = 73$ or that the sun revolves around the earth, even if you "believed it with all your heart." That's because you obviously know those things aren't true. And because you're a thinking person, you also know that merely saying something doesn't somehow make it true or real. Even *believing* something doesn't make it true. It's either true or not, independent of our belief in it.

Another reason truth is so critical to our faith is that it reflects the character and nature of God. God is true, and His Word is truth.[34] All truth is His. So when we pursue, discover, believe, and live out His truth, we honor Him and exalt His character.

Sound doctrine is also important to us because believing something that is *un*true about God is idolatry. We typically step into this trap when we believe or entertain a subtle or blatant lie about God. This is essentially substituting biblical truth about Him with our own. Therefore, what we believe about God, Christ, heaven, and the Christian life is not elective but essential. To be apathetic about belief confines us to a state of immaturity and destines us for spiritual impotence. And no disciple of Christ wants that.

We must also allow Scripture to inform and influence our beliefs, because our thinking is inherently limited and flawed. God understands this, so the Holy Spirit in us partners with the Word of God, illuminating His truth and moving us toward maturity in our thinking, character, and behavior.[35]

Lastly, sound doctrine shields us against Satan's deceptive lies and half-truths. The more truth we know and personally engage, the more protected we will be in the midst of spiritual warfare. This prevents us from being deceived by the devil's many schemes.[36] If we are to effectively contend for the faith in this world, we must be men and women who know *what* and *why* we believe. This is God's call on every Christian.[37]

DETECTING COUNTERFEITS

Doctrinal discernment is a spiritual life skill you learn over time, not in a single sermon or book. It acts like perpetual faith radar, sounding an internal alarm whenever Scripture is being misrepresented or compromised.

Imagine for a moment you were training to become a pilot. You would expect to log hundreds of hours in classes and receive personal instruction from an experienced pilot, right? Then there would be many hours of in-flight training and multiple test runs long before you ever took a solo flight. You wouldn't assume you could fly a fighter jet just because you watched *Top Gun* a few times! You wouldn't buy a sweatshirt that says, "Harvard Law School" and then expect to argue a case before a judge and jury, would you?

However, that's pretty close to what happened in the case of a teenager named Frank Abagnale. Devastated by his parents' divorce in 1963, Frank channeled his disappointment and frustration by birthing an elaborate con scheme, successfully posing as an airline pilot. He also masqueraded as a lawyer and even a doctor. All along the way, Abagnale funded his ruse by forging checks, which soon totaled millions of dollars. Eventually caught, he spent years in French, Swiss, and American prisons before being offered a chance to work for the FBI's Bank Fraud Division. His story was so incredible it was adapted into a movie called *Catch Me If You Can*, starring Tom Hanks and Leonardo DiCaprio. But even though people called Frank Abagnale "Captain" and "Doctor," he was neither. He was in reality an imposter. A deceiver. A fake. And he knew all along what he was doing.

Unfortunately, many today misrepresent God and Scripture, all the while believing they're speaking the truth. There are, to be sure, those who intentionally deceive others for power and profit. Other false teachers are sincere and confident, even though what they spout is pure heresy. But sincerity is no substitute for biblical integrity. From online webcasts, blogs, and television appearances to church pulpits and Barnes & Noble bookshelves, apostasy by any other name smells just as rotten.

That may sound a bit harsh and restrictive, maybe even confining or narrow-minded. If it sounds this way, it's because it is.

Read Jesus' words in Matthew 7:13-14: "You can enter God's Kingdom only through the narrow gate. The highway to hell is broad, and its gate is wide for the many who choose that way. But the gateway to life is very narrow and the road is difficult, and only a few ever find it" (NLT).

Interestingly enough, the Lord's very next words warn about false teachers: "Beware of false prophets who come disguised as harmless sheep but are really vicious wolves. You can identify them by their fruit, that is, by the way they act."[38]

Without a clear understanding of Scripture and a constant calibration of our hearts and minds to God's Word, the truth in us can fade and even morph to accommodate our feelings or the changing times. So how can the average Christian tell the difference between counterfeit truth and the real thing? How can you know if a pastor, teacher, speaker, blogger, or author is speaking the truth about God and the Bible? How can you detect false doctrine?

The good news is that we can know whose message is false and whose isn't, even when the teachers are all dressed like us sheep. We do this by examining their teachings and the fruit of their ministries. Does what they say square up with the Word? Does it harmonize with a historical understanding of Bible doctrine? What do their ministries generally produce—disciples of Jesus or spiritual "groupies"? Even someone's personal testimony must be authenticated by Scripture.

This isn't to say any of us fully understands all that happened at the moment of salvation or that we're able to eloquently articulate it. But as we grow, we begin to grasp the deep well of truth behind something as simple as trusting Christ for salvation. Otherwise, someone can claim almost anything about God or a personal experience with Him, and unless you've trained your mind, you can easily be misled or mistaught by persuasive words, emotion, and a compelling presentation. But when you are a student of the Bible, God's thoughts over time become embedded in your thinking. Scripture then acts like a "truth filtering system," sifting out Satan's clever lies. This kind of discernment is further developed and sharpened by walking the narrow road in the companionship of the One who personifies Truth.[39]

For five years, I (Jeff) lived in Mobile, Alabama, where

I served as student pastor at a local church. During that time, we held youth events on the USS *Alabama*, a World War II battleship. Permanently docked in Mobile Bay, the *Alabama* is one of that state's top tourist attractions. We rented out the entire ship, and our students had fun exploring its many features, as well as enjoying some healthy competition, after which I would speak on spiritual warfare. However, during one of our visits, a girl began complaining of being seasick.

"It's all the rocking back and forth of the ship," she said. "I don't know how much more I can take."

In my attempt to calm her down, I carefully explained that the *Alabama* wasn't really rocking back and forth as she had thought. The 42,000-ton ship's hull was securely resting on the bottom of Mobile Bay, permanently anchored in concrete. The ship wasn't actually rocking at all. It was all in her mind.

Believer, your Bible is an immovable bedrock of truth, anchored in God Himself. And though your senses may make you feel like its truth is rocking back and forth, it nevertheless remains solid and eternal.

Martin Luther purportedly wrote,

Feelings come and feelings go,
And feelings are deceiving;
My warrant is the Word of God—
Naught else is worth believing.
Though all my heart should feel condemned
For want of some sweet token,

There is One greater than my heart
Whose Word cannot be broken.
I'll trust in God's unchanging Word
Till soul and body sever,
For, though all things shall pass away,
His Word shall stand forever!

Rest assured. Despite what culture or popular Christian thought may propose, God's truth does not change, progress, or emerge. And though it's not your job to correct the entire world regarding false teaching or to become the "doctrine police," you are still called to stand for and proclaim what is true, and even when necessary to expose false teaching and heresy.[40] Always ask, "What does the Bible say?" not "Does it make me feel good, happy, or accepted by others?" Evaluate others' truth claims, and trace your own beliefs back to Scripture.[41] This is your "true north," your compass in a confusing culture, your immovable bedrock in an ever-raging storm.[42]

CHAPTER 4

CULTURE OF COMPROMISE

ONE OF THE BEST-KNOWN tabletop games is Jenga. In this game of skill, wooden rectangles are stacked together to construct a tower. Players take turns removing one of the rectangles without causing the tower to fall. As blocks are removed, they are placed on top of the tower, so the structure gets progressively taller and less stable. Finally, someone pulls out a block, and the whole structure collapses and falls apart all over the table.

Many in the church today are playing theological Jenga. They're pulling out one doctrinal or moral truth after another, leaving gaping holes as the citadel of the faith grows less and less stable. But like a game of Jenga, eventually one key block is removed, and the structure can no longer stand. The whole thing collapses in a jumbled pile. Of course, no human opposition or distortion of the truth can ever bring down God's tower of truth, but in human terms, the visible church of Jesus Christ is weakening before our eyes.

The compromises we see today in the professing church are both doctrinal and moral. The doctrinal foundations of the faith—such as the inspiration and sufficiency of the Scriptures, the virgin birth of Jesus, the deity of Christ, forgiveness by grace alone through faith alone in Christ alone, and the literal, visible return of Jesus to earth—are no longer considered essential and in many cases are viewed as detrimental to progress. I'm reminded of a story from the ministry of Billy Graham. At the close of his early Los Angeles Crusade, his ministry and preaching was described in *Time* magazine by an Episcopalian rector, who was quoted as saying, "I believe he's putting the church back 50 years." At the ministers' breakfast during the closing week of the crusade, Graham, who rarely responded to his critics, said, "I'm afraid I've failed. I had hoped to put the church back 2,000 years."[1]

Along with the doctrinal departure from the truth, moral standards are being pulled out one after another like Jenga blocks. Francis Schaeffer pointed out this danger years ago: "If our reflex action is always accommodation regardless of the centrality of the truth involved, there is something wrong."[2]

William Booth (1829–1912), who founded the Salvation Army, was a passionate follower of Jesus Christ. On the eve of the twentieth century, Booth predicted that the gospel would not fare well in the new century. He predicted that by the end of the twentieth century, many in the church would be preaching

- Christianity without Christ,
- Forgiveness without repentance,
- Salvation without regeneration, and
- Heaven without hell.

Booth's words seem prophetic. That's exactly where we find ourselves today. As the saying goes, "The living faith of the dead has become the dead faith of the living." We see this all around us. Compromise has sucked the life out of the living faith. Many churchgoers yawn today over the truths for which their forefathers shed blood and even died.

Recent polls disclose that 70 percent of Americans with a religious affiliation say that many religions—not just their own—can lead to salvation and eternal life, while 57 percent of evangelical regular church attenders believe that many religions can bring salvation.[3] These statistics represent an unprecedented sea change in opinion. They show that the greatest danger to the church today is not humanism, paganism, atheism, or agnosticism. The greatest danger is not increasing hostility against our faith from the culture. Our greatest danger is apostasy on the inside, arising from false teachers—theological liberals who deny and distort biblical doctrine and lead others down the same path.

Christians often fear what's happening in our culture. We

fear what the government may do to our churches, and that concern is certainly not without justification. Yet we need to remember that in Revelation 2:5, it wasn't Caesar who would come close the doors of the church; it was Jesus Christ. Jesus would close the doors and vacate the premises. Jesus told the church at Ephesus that He would remove the lampstand of the church. He would pull the plug and turn out the lights. We mourn a decaying culture, and rightly so, but the greatest danger to our churches and to each of us individually is falling away from the truth of God's Word. As Vance Havner once said, "The biggest danger to the church is not woodpeckers on the outside, but termites on the inside." The termites of compromise gradually gnaw away at the insides of the church and individual lives, leaving empty shells behind.

Many today are openly, even militantly, against the truth, but others' stances are much more murky. Trying to discern their positions on key theological or moral issues is like nailing Jell-O to the wall. Their approach is akin to a theological smorgasbord. As I heard someone say recently, "Vague is now vogue." Yet either way, the church is now caving to pressure from the world.[4] How did we get here? Why is this happening? How do we regain our footing in a culture of downward-sliding values?

TWO KINDS OF COMPROMISE

For many today, compromise is easy. They have no problem compromising on many things, even essential Christian beliefs and morals. For others, *compromise* is a dirty word. In their view, nothing worthwhile should ever be compromised. The truth, it appears, lies in the middle of these extremes. Not all compromise is bad. Broadly speaking, there are two kinds of compromise—wise and worldly. Wise compromise is an attempt to find a way between two extremes. It gives up personal preferences and selfish desires for the sake of unity and peace. Wise compromise is good. We compromise all the time in marriage, family, business, and even politics. No one can have everything their way all the time. Many things in life can be compromised without violating any essential principle. Biblical submission—a willingness to yield to others, a lack of self-centeredness, and a concern with what others think—is a form of wise compromise.

Worldly compromise, on the other hand, is bad. It backs away from essential moral principles. It surrenders truth to error, morality to immorality, and good to evil. That's what's happening in many churches and entire denominations today. A.W. Tozer observes, "The blessing of God is promised to the peacemaker, but the religious negotiator had better watch his step. . . . Darkness and light can never be brought together by talk. Some things are not negotiable."[5]

The Old Testament prophet Daniel is an apt illustration for the balance between wise and worldly compromise. He and some of the other youth from the Jewish nobility were deported from Jerusalem to Babylon by King Nebuchadnezzar. Through his assistants, Nebuchadnezzar instituted a program to fully assimilate these young Israelites into Babylonian life and culture. The plan was to change their language, education, names, and diet. Daniel and his friends wisely agreed to many of the changes. They agreed to learn a new language. (After all, they needed to know the language of Babylon to get along.) They agreed to the three years of advanced education that probably involved mathematics, astrology, astronomy, and agriculture. They even agreed to change their names. Nothing in the law prevented them from taking Babylonian names. But when it came to the matter of diet, they refused to change.[6] Why? Because God had given clear dietary restrictions in the law. The food Nebuchadnezzar presented to them had been offered to idols as a sacrifice and violated the proscriptions in the law. That's where Daniel and his friends drew the line. Daniel would not change, compromise, or concede—even in the face of death. He had convictions based on God's Word. There's an old saying: "Great doors swing on small hinges." Daniel's refusal to compromise God's truth was the small hinge on which the great door of his life would swing.

Years ago, G. K. Chesterton made this powerful statement: "The object of opening the mind, as of opening the mouth, is to shut it again on something solid." Those who have trusted in the gospel—the Good News of Jesus Christ— have closed their minds on the solid truth that He is God in human flesh who provides the only way to God the Father and that life must be ordered according to God's Word, the Bible. These convictions can never be compromised. We can compromise on many things in life, and we are wise to do so, but we are not to be open minded when it comes to the gospel and its implications for daily life.

In the musical *Fiddler on the Roof*, Tevye is a loving father who is confronted, one at a time, with things his children want to do that displease him. He at first denies them, but when he is alone, he begins to weigh both sides of the issue. He says to himself, "On the one hand . . ." as he considers the aspects of one side of the issue. Then he says to himself, "But on the other hand . . ." as he lists other factors involved. He then grants the child's request, even though it goes against his wishes. But when one of his daughters wants to marry a young Russian communist, he forbids her. As he begins to reason with himself in his common pattern of "On the one hand . . ." and "On the other hand . . . ," he cannot allow it. In this instance, he says, "There is no 'other hand.'"

That is true when we come to the faith. There are some nonnegotiables in the Christian life. When it comes to the gospel of Jesus Christ and the moral implications that flow from it, there is no "on the other hand."

WHY SO MUCH COMPROMISE AND APOSTASY?

One thoughtful question to ask at this point is, Why is there so much compromise today and an epidemic of apostasy? Why are so many falling away, apparently so quickly and easily? Why are biblical essentials being jettisoned so casually? What leads people within the church to depart from the truth of God's Word? Of course, many reasons and rationales could be given, but these five seem to stand out in Scripture.

The first three are fairly straightforward and simple. We will spend more time examining the final two. First, many compromise out of love for the world—plain and simple. They love their sin and don't want to follow God's Word.[7] They substitute God's wisdom with their own. They put themselves above the Bible rather than under it. Second, others compromise because of superficial attention to God's Word. They don't know the Bible and don't take it seriously. They drift away from the truth.[8] Third, compromise can sometimes result from all-out, blatant rebellion and defiance.[9]

Fourth, many compromise because the Bible and the words of Jesus can be hard and narrow. Jesus often lost followers because His teachings were too hard.[10] His words rub against the grain of our sinful nature. For this reason, compromising beliefs or behavior makes it much easier to live self-centered lives and avoid any clash with the world around us. In his early life, Mark Twain moved to a mining town in Nevada. It was a wide-open town with brothels and bars on every corner. Twain said, "I immediately recognized it was no place for a Presbyterian, so I decided not to be one." He compromised. Many have followed his example. Finding it hard to be a Christian, they either quit trying or compromise their convictions.

Fifth, many want to please people. They can't stand to be mocked, maligned, and mistreated. The allure of acceptance is strong. Taking the broad road and fitting in is less stressful.

Swimming upstream is difficult and tiring. Compromise always lowers the standard. It's seldom offensive. It tells people what they want to hear, which is why it's so appealing. Telling people they can believe whatever they want and live however they want is much more comfortable than telling people the truth, even though only the truth can really set them free.

We in the church today are under constant pressure to weaken our theology and our morality to make people feel good. We hear things like "You don't have to believe the gospel of Jesus Christ to go to heaven. There are many roads to heaven." Or "Nobody will go to hell. Hell is not a literal place." Or "God's will is for you to be rich and healthy all the time." Or "You can love who you want to love. God will never judge you. He's all about love." Or "Why believe in a book written so long ago?"

The rising tide of progressivism is applauded by many like John Shore:

> It is inevitable that liberal/progressive Christians will be the majority of Christians in America. We feel the waters of that sea change already swelling everywhere around us. Today's conservative evangelical Christians who are rallying against "postmodern relativism," "revisionist secular theology," "a naturalistic doctrine of God," or however else they might label the theology of the left, are like yesteryear's horse-and-buggy owners rallying against them dangnabit newfangled automobiles.[11]

Unbeknownst to him, Shore's sentiments are actually prophesied in Scripture. His attitude fulfills what the Bible says will prevail in the last days. The apostle Paul's final charge to his protégé Timothy prophesies what we see today:

> I solemnly charge you in the presence of God and of Christ Jesus, who is to judge the living and the dead, and by His appearing and His kingdom: preach the word; be ready in season and out of season; reprove, rebuke, exhort, with great patience and instruction. For the time will come when they will not endure sound doctrine; but wanting to have their ears tickled, they will accumulate for themselves teachers in accordance to their own desires, and will turn away their ears from the truth and will turn aside to myths.[12]

Ear-tickling sermons are rampant today. As Tim LaHaye and Jerry Jenkins write,

> False teachers rarely exist in a spiritual vacuum. They start appearing because people want to hear and act on their flesh-stroking doctrines. In many ways, spirituality is as much a commodity as is electronics or beef and is subject to similar laws of supply and demand. . . . In other words, the people demand to hear ungodly fables, and soon false teachers start appearing to supply the demand—like flies to a garbage dump.[13]

A consistent mantra of contemporary apostates is their concern that Christians today will be hated or doomed to irrelevance if we stand for the truth. If we want to win the world, we have to tell them what they want to hear, caving to their cravings, compromising our convictions so that others will be more enticed to join us. The most important virtue is not offending anyone. But if that's our goal, we have to raise the question—what are we converting people to?

Ironically, those calling for compromise and no offense in areas of sexual morality won't hesitate to berate Christians for their greed, selfishness, and lack of care for the poor. When it comes to pressing social justice issues on Christians, they quote the Bible literally and assume a no-holds-barred approach. They pull no punches when it comes to certain kinds of sinful behavior. Yet when it comes to homosexuality and other culturally accepted sins, we have to put on pillow-sized boxing gloves and pull all our punches lest anyone take the slightest degree of offense. As Doc Holliday says to his friend Wyatt Earp near the end of the movie *Tombstone*, "My hypocrisy knows no bounds."

Theological liberals and progressives also employ the tactics of shame and humiliation. They claim the moral high ground and look down on conservative, Bible-believing Christians as unloving, negative, and nasty. Yet when we disagree with them and their take on Scripture, we are immediately labeled as bigots and haters and accused of suffering from one phobia or another. We can't be allowed to have an honest disagreement with their view. We have to be branded, vilified, and castigated for our position. But no matter how loudly they denounce our stand on God's Word, we cannot allow fear of shame or humiliation to cause us to cower and compromise.

DO WE HAVE A STANDARD?

While many modern theological progressives have a low view of Scripture, they do appeal to it at times to support their views while at the same time discounting the parts they don't like. One of their favorite passages is John 8—the story about the woman caught in adultery, who was brought to Jesus by His enemies. This beautiful story is twisted to support all kinds of unbiblical notions of moral compromise. Rachel Held Evans, for example, believes Jesus broke the law of God to help the woman in this story. She writes,

> Jesus once said that his mission was not to abolish the law, but to fulfill it. And in this instance, fulfilling the law meant letting it go. It may serve as little comfort to those who have suffered abuse at the hand of Bible-wielding literalists, but the disturbing laws of Leviticus and Deuteronomy lose just a bit of their potency when God himself breaks them.[14]

This is a not-so-subtle discounting of the validity and authority of the Bible and a blasphemous charge that Jesus sinned. However, Evans misses the point. J. Carl Laney provides helpful insight into the meaning of this text:

Yet, the law that required death for the adulteress also demanded that qualified witnesses be the first to begin the stoning (Deut. 17:7). Were these witnesses qualified according to the requirements of the Mosaic Law?

Jesus' words "If any of you is without sin" refer to the key qualification in the Mosaic law, namely that the witnesses be nonmalicious (Deut. 19:16-19, 21; cf. Ex. 23:1-8). A malicious witness promotes violence, perverts justice, and misuses the law for selfish purposes, precisely what the religious leaders were doing in this case. Jesus knew that those testifying against the women were not doing so out of pure hearts and a concern for right. Their conspiracy, inequity, and selfish purposes disqualified them from participation in the execution called for by Mosaic law. . . . Jesus was not applying "situation ethics." He called adultery sin and commanded the woman to cease sinning. Jesus was not relaxing the moral standards of God. Rather He was carefully applying the law. The law called for stoning, but it also required that the witnesses be qualified.[15]

Another way to view this incident is that "Jesus is not breaking the law or shrugging off the Old Testament law. Rather, Jesus is calling these men out on their double-standard, thinking the law applied more to adulterous [women] than to adulterous men."[16] In either case, there is no need to view Jesus as a law-breaking compromiser as Held Evans suggests. The grace and forgiveness Jesus extended to the woman in John 8 should not be used to soften Jesus' stance against sin. We have to remember that after saving her life, Jesus famously said to her, "Go and sin no more," which in the context refers to the sin of adultery.[17]

Notice Jesus didn't whitewash her sin. He called it what it was. Additionally, the same Jesus who rescued the woman in John 8 from the murderous mob told his followers one chapter earlier that the world "hate[s] me because I accuse it of doing evil."[18] Later in John's Gospel Jesus says,

> If the world hates you, remember that it hated me
> first. The world would love you as one of its own
> if you belonged to it, but you are no longer part of
> the world. I chose you to come out of the world,
> so it hates you. Do you remember what I told you?
> "A slave is not greater than the master." Since they
> persecuted me, naturally they will persecute you.
> And if they had listened to me, they would listen to
> you. They will do all this to you because of me, for
> they have rejected the one who sent me. They would
> not be guilty if I had not come and spoken to them.
> But now they have no excuse for their sin. Anyone
> who hates me also hates my Father.[19]

We must not take Jesus or any of Scripture in bits and pieces, divorced from the overall context. Yes, sexual sins are not the only sins in the Bible. Injustice and greed are sins, and we must never shy away from naming them. But none of us can choose our favorite sins to condemn and let others slide out of fear that we will become unpopular with the world.

I have to admit that we all use Jesus sometimes to support our pet views while at the same time ignoring what He says about our own sinful habits and attitudes. None of us are without blame in using Jesus or other parts of Scripture for our own agendas. But let's at least be honest about how prone we are to misuse Scripture and do the best we can to interpret the words of Jesus and all of the words of Scripture fairly, accurately, and completely in their original context. Anything less is unacceptable.

LET ME ILLUSTRATE

To help you see the depth of the doctrinal confusion and compromise today, here's one example of thousands that could be cited from the blogosphere. The author of this blog is a *New York Times* bestselling author, and her online community is visited by hundreds of thousands of readers every day:

> The better way, the underneath perfection of things that I feel deep in my bones looks like this: There is no war. All hungry people are fed. All lonely people are loved. . . . People of all races, religions, genders, sexualities, cultures, and abilities are valued equally

in our one human family. There is Justice. Peace. Love. Equality.

This sort of unseen order of things—in my view—is heaven on Earth. Christians might call it the Kingdom of God. My Jewish friends call it Shalom while my atheist friends call it Love or Peace. Lovingkindness. Our Buddhist brothers and sisters might call it. [sic] ALL PEOPLE who are working to bring the above unseen order of things to Earth now—whether they are atheist, Jewish, Buddhist, Hindu, Muslim, or Christian—THESE people are my faith partners. I don't really care what label you give yourself, I care about the unseen order of things you believe in and are working towards. . . .

But if we want a little scripture to support the idea of disregarding labels—we could look at Matthew 7:21. "Not everyone who calls out to me, 'Lord! Lord!' will enter the Kingdom of Heaven. Only those who actually do the will of my Father in heaven will enter."

Do I think this scripture is a threat of hell? Hell no. I don't think any scripture is a threat—I think scripture is an invitation into an unseen order of things that is truer than anything we can actually see.[20]

Notice the repeated language of "feeling" and "what I think." Feeling and human opinion is the modern Bible. The author does appeal to Matthew 7:21 and believes it does not refer to people being judged, yet ironically the entire context of Matthew 7:15-23 concerns false shepherds who lead unsuspecting sheep away from the narrow path that leads to salvation and down the broad road that leads to destruction. What the author is doing in her blog tragically fulfills the stern warning of Jesus in the very passage she quotes. This blogger joins the chorus of voices who deny and disregard the inerrancy and sufficiency of Scripture and the exclusivity of Jesus as the way to God.

Many would claim that compromise on these issues is harmless and benign. They wonder why all the fuss over a few theological points. For them the words *doctrine* or *doctrinal* are pejoratives. They view doctrinal, theological truths as irrelevant, impractical, divisive, unloving, and even unknowable. The problem is that they have no love for these truths or appreciation for the dire, eternal consequences that hang in the balance. Jesus spoke often of the eternal destruction of those who reject Him and His teaching.[21]

I like the story about the New York family that bought a ranch out West where they intended to raise cattle. Friends visited and asked if the ranch had a name. "Well," said the would-be cattleman, "I wanted to name it the Bar-J. My wife favored Suzy-Q, one son liked the Flying-W, and the other wanted the Lazy-Y. So we're calling it the Bar-J-Suzy-Q-Flying-W-Lazy-Y Ranch."

"But where are all your cattle?" the friends asked.

The reply: "None survived the branding." Make no mistake: compromise can be deadly!

FAITHFUL PEOPLE

When confronted by apostasy, I find solace in tracing the lives of great saints from the past who stood in their day against a similar tide and refused to compromise even in the face of withering opposition. One of these faithful people was Athanasius of Alexandria. The life of Athanasius is an epic saga. He served as bishop of Alexandria for forty-five years. He knew five popes and five emperors. He survived five exiles—nearly twenty years—as well as persecution under Emperor Diocletian.

Athanasius is best known for his lengthy battle against the heresy of Arianism. Arius, a church leader from Alexandria, Egypt, believed that Jesus was not coequal and coeternal with God the Father and claimed that Jesus was a created being. He taught that Christ the Son was simply a creature—the greatest of all created beings. Athanasius didn't shrug off the issue as unimportant or inconsequential. He understood that the entire Christian faith was at stake. The controversy with Arias raged on for several years. At one point, when it looked like the entire Roman Empire was moving away from orthodoxy into Arianism, a concerned, exasperated colleague of Athanasius exclaimed, "The whole world is against you!" Unfazed, Athanasius made this famous response, "Then it is Athanasius against the world."

Another early giant of the faith was Tertullian, a lawyer from Carthage (in North Africa) who served the church in the third century. He authored a book titled *On Idolatry*. The book deals with the issue of Christians who made a living by making idols. When believers in his day were told that because they were Christians they should not be involved in the business of making idols, they said, "We have to live. There's no other way by which we can live."

Tertullian's response was "Do you have to live?"

What a probing question. It cuts to the heart of compromise. We always have some excuse for our compromise. The ultimate justification would be "I have to live." Yet the truth is, you and I do not. We *think* we have to live. Many today believe that they have to live and even have to live a comfortable life without any clash with our culture. The truth is, however, you and I *don't* have to live. The ultimate claim upon our lives is loyalty to Christ. Our ultimate loyalty is not to our physical life—it's to Christ. We don't have to live, but we do have to be loyal to Him. That's what life is all about.

As leaders, churches, and denominations swerve from the truth and increasingly fall away, we need to stand like Daniel, like Athanasius, and like Tertullian for the truth of God's Word. No matter how strong and sustained the opposition may grow, we must joyfully, graciously stand for the truth, lovingly share it with others, and strive to live it out in our lives every day by the power of the Holy Spirit.

CHAPTER 5

WHEN TOLERANCE IS INTOLERABLE

I have this against you, that you tolerate the woman Jezebel.

REVELATION 2:20

March 16 2017

AMERICAN AIRLINES FLIGHT 11 pushed back from gate 26 in what was expected to be a routine flight from Boston to Los Angeles. Captain John Ogonowski and his Boeing 767-200ER taxied down the runway with nine flight attendants and eighty-one passengers on board and took off at 7:59 a.m. No one could have dreamed that forty-seven minutes later, they would all be dead. When the airliner rocketed into the World Trade Center's North Tower at 440 mph, 9,717 gallons of jet fuel exploded, catapulting everyone aboard into eternity.

The whole world changed in an instant.

What precipitated the events of that disastrous September day was a mere handful of men. Consumed by a jihadist ideology, they had committed themselves to the destruction of human life. And so, storming their way into the cockpit, they took control of Flight 11 while simultaneously attacking and killing passengers and crew.

The ringleader of this unholy war from the sky that day was Egyptian terrorist Mohamed Atta. He was accompanied by four fellow terrorists (all from Saudi Arabia). When the body count was totaled, 1,466 additional persons perished in the North Tower, with another 624 in the South Tower. American passenger jets transformed into explosive missiles manned by maniacal Muslims. It was the worst hijacking in history. And though sudden and unexpected, it had actually been years in the making.

In these last days, it's not just planes that are being hijacked. The Bible claims, "The human heart is the most deceitful of all things, and desperately wicked. Who really knows how bad it is?"[1]

Because humanity is inherently depraved, we initiate and participate in other types of hijackings: kidnapping truth, moral values, and even common sense. Through crafty deception over time, our sin nature, partnering with the spirit of the age, takes hostage the good things of God in an attempt to redefine, reimagine, and in some cases wipe them completely from humanity's hard drive.

We're seeing this pirating of morals and standards occur today as it relates to the concept of *love*. Seeking to justify homosexual activity and same-sex marriage, LGBT activists coined the catchphrase "Love Is Love." The argument behind this slogan is that if any person feels romantic affection or attraction toward any other person (regardless of their gender or age), then of course it *must* be love, right? Hence "Love Is Love." Admittedly, if you redefine what *love* is, as well as from where it originates, then virtually any definition or expression of this love immediately becomes legitimate and justifiable. *Morally* right. Even a "human right." Redefined and viewed this way, love itself is no longer a definitive standard by which all mankind should operate but rather an ever-evolving whim birthed out of individual preference. Marital and sexual love then become affections and emotions one can feel for anyone—other men or women, even multiple persons involving multiple genders or no "gender" at all. *Each person* (that is to say, each deceitful, wicked heart) decides what love is, not some ancient book or supposed deity.

Of course, if there is truly no God or authoritative Scripture, then logically there is no ultimate standard for morality—or for reality, in that case. What is "good" or "right" for you is just as valid as anyone else's choices. For with no God to create, reveal, guide, judge, or reward, then everyone's life decisions are equally credible . . . and meaningless.

By the same token, with no God, there can also be no authoritative or conclusive way to know whether what you feel for someone else is a genuine spiritual connection, an emotional feeling, or a social compulsion. There's no way to determine if "love" is merely a physical urge brought on by chemicals. If we are just "molecules in motion," we are incapable of knowing *anything* for certain. As C. S. Lewis wisely observed,

> Supposing there was no intelligence behind the universe, no creative mind. In that case, nobody designed my brain for the purpose of thinking. It is merely that when the atoms inside my skull happen, for physical or chemical reasons, to arrange themselves in a certain way, this gives me, as a byproduct, the sensation I call thought. But, if so, how can I trust my own thinking to be true? It's like upsetting a milk jug and hoping that the way it splashes itself will give you a map of London. But if I can't trust my own thinking, of course I can't trust the arguments leading to Atheism, and therefore have no reason to be an Atheist, or anything else. Unless I believe in God, I cannot believe in thought: so I can never use thought to disbelieve in God.[2]

So then, there cannot even be such a thing as "real love" without God. Moreover, Scripture tells us the following:

- "We know what real love is because Jesus gave up his life for us."[3]
- "This is how God loved the world: He gave his one and only Son, so that everyone who believes in him will not perish but have eternal life."[4]

- "God showed his great love for us by sending Christ to die for us while we were still sinners."[5]

The Bible also unquestionably asserts that love *comes from* God. So then, love is not love; *God* is.[6] Further, the only way we can truly know love in any kind of meaningful relationship is by first experiencing His love for us.[7] And this is nowhere more true than in the marriage relationship. As a husband and wife experience God's love, they are able to experience a deeper love for each other.[8]

Of course, non-Christians can experience some aspects of love. They can perform unselfish acts of service on behalf of others. They can know the emotional bliss and satisfaction of having another person in their lives. They can appreciate how that person fills a void where loneliness once dwelled. They can enjoy the wonderful companionship of human relational love. However, they can never fully experience all that love is and has to offer until they receive it from the God who is love.

Finally, a person cannot give away what they do not personally possess. Encountering God's unconditional love and salvation gives believers a capacity for emotional fulfillment, selfless service, perseverance, and forgiveness that is exponentially enhanced beyond what the average person can know. Sadly, many professing Christians do not "grow in the grace and knowledge of our Lord and Savior Jesus Christ"[9] so as to deepen their exposure to His love and participation in it.

But what we are seeing happen today is more than just people missing out on God's love. Instead, there has been a deliberate, conscious movement to reject the biblical definition of love and marriage, replacing it with one that better harmonizes with culture's crumbling moral standards.

Following the US Supreme Court's 2014 ruling in favor of same-sex marriage, Starbucks flew a 38-foot-wide by 19-foot-tall "pride flag" over its corporate headquarters in Seattle. Anthony Hesseltine, a senior operations buyer for Starbucks, remarked at the time, "The whole message is about diversity and accepting people for their differences. If you think about a rainbow, no one color is dominant. It's a harmonization of different colors, each color contributing to the whole."[10]

Diversity and harmony. And two more hijackings.

Our society is bowing at the altar of tolerance and worshiping at the shrine of open-mindedness. Values that have historically been championed by the Christian faith are systematically being replaced, treated like burned-out lightbulbs by a culture that's in a romantic relationship with darkness.[11] Think of how our world is redefining the following Christian concepts:

- Acceptance (Romans 15:7)
- Unity and diversity (Galatians 3:27-29; 1 Corinthians 12:12-13)
- Compassion (Colossians 3:12-13)
- Justice (Proverbs 28:5; 29:7; Micah 6:8; Romans 12:19)
- Spirituality (Matthew 5:21-28; Galatians 5:16; Ephesians 5:18)
- Bigotry and prejudice (Acts 10:28; Romans 10:12-13; Colossians 3:11; James 2:9)

- Hatred (Proverbs 6:16-19; Romans 12:9)
- Forgiveness (Ephesians 4:32; Colossians 3:13;
  1 Thessalonians 5:15)
- Truth (John 4:24; 8:32; 14:6; 17:17)
- Martyrdom (Matthew 10:28; Luke 11:50-51;
  Hebrews 11:37-40; Revelation 2:10; 6:11)

When comparing the way each of these concepts is defined in culture with Scripture's description of them, you can see how they have been twisted and fashioned into weapons against those who follow Jesus. It's a turning of the tables, a changing of the price tags. And it's a modern-day example of the prophet Isaiah's words:

Woe to those who call evil good, and good evil.
Who substitute darkness for light and light for darkness;
Who substitute bitter for sweet, and sweet for bitter! [12]

Paul echoed Isaiah, writing that those who deliberately reject the Creator and His right to rule in their lives "exchange the truth of God for a lie." The consequence of this spiritual rebellion is that God "gives them over" to judgment. [13] And humanity continues devolving deeper into the depths of depravity, to the point where they

became full of every kind of wickedness, sin, greed, hate, envy, murder, quarreling, deception, malicious behavior, and gossip. They are backstabbers, haters

of God, insolent, proud, and boastful. They invent
new ways of sinning, and they disobey their parents.
They refuse to understand, break their promises,
are heartless, and have no mercy. They know God's
justice requires that those who do these things
deserve to die, yet they do them anyway. Worse yet,
they encourage others to do them, too.[14]

TELLING THE TRUTH

So we can see from Scripture that many of today's promoted
values and "truths" are nothing more than lies, reimagined
imitations of the real thing. *Hate* has been redefined to mean
"your biblical values clash with mine; therefore, you are a
hater." Ironically, what the world now calls "hate" is met with
actual hate in return. But this is nothing new. The same thing
happened in Jesus' day. Our Lord demonstrated more love
toward sinners than anyone ever could. And yet motivated by
this same (real) love, He also told the truth to those who were
unrepentant regarding their sin. And they, in turn, vehemently
hated Him for it.[15] It's also part of what got Him killed.

Some Christians will use the popular "Jesus hung out with
sinners" argument to justify friendships or to tolerate sin in
the body of Christ. And though believers should always seek
to build bridges and friendships with the lost, what sometimes escapes our notice is that many of those sinners Christ
spent time with were keenly aware that their sinful condition and their condemnable lifestyles posed a problem. Yes,

Jesus accepted them into His presence, but He did not accept them into His *Kingdom* until they acknowledged their need for Him and trusted Him to forgive their sins. It is these He promises to "never reject."[16]

So in these last days, Scripture's values and virtues have been hijacked by a post-Christian civilization birthed and fed by Satanic delusion and darkened hearts and minds. In fact, nothing appears to be sacred anymore in a world ramping up to Revelation. Morals, values, virtues, origins, sexuality— all are up for grabs, recycled and resold to those whose consciences are not cleansed by Scripture. Even the rainbow we see in the sky has been taken hostage and redefined to symbolize the various gender, sex, and relationship choices currently promoted and celebrated in our age.

Nevertheless, God made the rainbow, and it has absolutely nothing to do with sexuality. It does, however, have symbolic meaning, a sign of a promise God made to Noah and to successive generations that He would never destroy humanity with water again.[17] Ironically, this promise came after He had brought devastating global judgment on mankind because of the godlessness, violence, and moral corruption that now fills our planet![18]

THE "UNPARDONABLE SIN"

But perhaps the biggest hijacking of all is what our culture has done to "tolerance." The way some people talk, you'd think tolerance is the most important virtue. In the spirit of tolerance, some colleges and universities have now created "safe spaces" on their campuses to "protect" students from divergent opinions. So, for example, if you claim to be transgender, lesbian, or "otherkin" (those who identify as partially or totally nonhuman—like a dragon or a fox), then the school will provide a space where you can be protected from shame, ridicule, oppression, or persecution.[19] Yes, *persecution*. Clearly, humanity has taken a Romans 1 turn for the bizarre. What is marketed and sold as tolerance today hardly resembles its corresponding Christian virtue.

In contemporary society, tolerance means being open to divergent ideas and being completely accepting of those who aren't like you. Sounds good, right? Even *Christian*-like. I mean, who wouldn't want to be known as open and accepting?

Those who are faithful Christ-followers already are. Christian tolerance means we demonstrate patience with non-Christian coworkers, classmates, friends, and family. It means we listen and care. We exercise tolerance because we love people and know God can change people. We pray for them and are patient toward them because we remember a time when God and others treated us with the same kind of tolerance.[20] It means they can come to God just as they are. After all, *we* did.

But along with compassion, understanding, and empathy, there is also a time to call sin what it is. As believers, we serve in a dual role of both priest and prophet, being both compassionate and confrontational. And though balancing that role can be challenging, the two responsibilities can exist together at the same time. We can be tolerant yet simultaneously unwavering toward God's Word. One may sound more "loving" than the other. But is it?

When my (Jeff's) son Stuart was two years old, his older brother accidentally fell on top of him, breaking his collarbone. The incident also broke my heart as we were all playing together when it happened. Psalm 103:13 says, "As a father has compassion on his children, so the LORD has compassion on those who fear Him." I felt that while driving Stuart to the hospital. And during his recovery, nobody exhibited more compassion for Stuart than I did. Every time I saw him wincing in pain, my heart ached. I wished so badly that I could have taken his suffering and discomfort away. But my compassion could not overrule the fact that he still needed to go to the doctor, to be examined and X-rayed, to have his arm placed in an uncomfortable sling, and to constantly be told to remain immobile for weeks to come. The cold, hard truth was that he would have to endure some tough days ahead. And as his father, I didn't just cuddle him and help him get dressed, but I also had to deny his requests to go outside and play.

That's because truth and compassion are not enemies. They're partners. And one without the other often leads to a misrepresentation of both. As Christians, we have a tendency to pendulum swing when it comes to dealing with the outside world. In our attempt to reach the lost, we can try so hard to be relevant that we compromise the truth.

Conversely, in "standing for what we believe," we can also commit the error of the Pharisees, neglecting "the weightier matters of the law: justice and mercy and faithfulness."[21] But none of God's attributes—from His amazing grace to His terrifying wrath—are ever mutually exclusive. They never conflict with or contradict themselves. It is only our limited understanding of those attributes that creates confusion. However, in God's economy, there is perfect harmony and divine balance among them all.

In practice, both the world and the church tend to upset that balance by overemphasizing one to the exclusion of the rest. What we need is a proper understanding of Scripture's values and virtues and skill in applying them to real-life people and circumstances.

Yes, because of truth, there is a time for unwavering intolerance. Parents have to display intolerance toward certain behaviors and attitudes in their children. Pastors must be intolerant of false doctrine and anyone who might threaten the well-being of their sheep. Husbands are intolerant of things that may harm their wives or marriages. Governments ought to be intolerant of evildoers, administering just punishment. And as Christians, we must show intolerance toward any thought, philosophy, or value that raises itself up against the knowledge of God.[22] In all these cases, intolerance isn't hatred or bigotry but genuine love, care, fairness, and justice.

Paul was intolerant of blatant sin in the church, pronouncing swift and thorough condemnation of those who participated in it in 1 Corinthians 5:1-7. However, just three verses later, he reminds the Corinthians to continue their friendships with unbelievers who are immoral, covetous, swindlers, and even idolaters. In this sense, we should never allow the world to outlove us. At the same time, Paul urged the Corinthians to limit fellowship with so-called "believers" who practice such sins. That's an example of how truth and love coexist in harmony with one another. Sadly, however, many in the Christian community are embracing this rede-fined tolerance, even reading and reinterpreting the Bible in light of it. And perhaps nowhere is this more blatant than when it comes to the sin of homosexuality. While Mark covers this issue more comprehensibly in chapter 7, it is worth noting that influential bloggers and authors like Matthew Vines have openly accepted and promoted homosexuality as not only tolerable but as coming from God Himself! The idea is that since homosexuals are all "born that way," Christians should accept, and even endorse, homosexual practice.

How ironic is it that our world (and some who claim to know Jesus) allows tolerance for everything *except* the Christian worldview? Where does this indiscriminate toler-ance mind-set come from? And more important, where is it taking us? How does a believer make sense of a culture that equates unbridled tolerance with love, even calling it *God's* love? This is where hijacked spiritual values especially pervert and twist biblical truths. They are reckless inclusion, careless love, and morals devoid of wisdom. These are the open gates through which apostasy enters. And we cannot and should not ever rely on human government to acknowledge God and support His standards.

Christian tolerance means making room in our hearts for those who are different from us. It also means accepting those who are weak in the faith or who have yet to mature in their relationship with God.[23] But as with any other virtue, it is tempered with wisdom. There are boundaries to how much tolerance we exhibit and for how long. We might tolerate our neighbor's barking dog for a few hours but not for an entire evening. We can tolerate a coworker's dissenting opinion but not when it begins to hinder productivity or company morale. We can tolerate a relative's negative opinion of us but not when that relative begins infecting others with lies and unfounded rumors. And we can tolerate people who are enslaved by sin yet never tolerate the sin itself.

However, unless we're careful, we can be guilty of the same sin as the church at Thyatira, one of five Revelation congregations to receive a blistering rebuke from Jesus. This community of faith overflowed with tolerance—the *bad* kind.

While Jesus praised the church at Ephesus because they did *not* "tolerate evil people," He then condemned the church at Thyatira *because* of their tolerance.[24] The Thyatiran believers happily coexisted with a woman in their church (nicknamed "Jezebel"), who referred to herself as a prophetess. Her teaching led the congregation away from holy living and into immorality and the "deep things of Satan."[25] And Christ was not pleased.

So we dare not have this attitude toward God's grace, abusing it for our own selfish pleasures.[26] But on the flip side of being libertine is what legalists do to God's commands, twisting, redefining, and reassigning more meaning to them than Scripture does, "teaching as doctrines the precepts of men."[27] Jesus sternly warned the Pharisees of His day, "Isaiah was right when he prophesied about you hypocrites; as it is written: 'These people honor me with their lips, but their hearts are far from me.'"[28] And again, "Woe to you, scribes and Pharisees, hypocrites! For you are like whitewashed tombs which on the outside appear beautiful, but inside they are full of dead men's bones and all uncleanness. So you, too, outwardly appear righteous to men, but inwardly you are full of hypocrisy and lawlessness."[29]

Legalists hijack the Christian concept of obedience, terrorizing God's people with it. This is actually a form of worldliness and carnality, because it feeds and enables the sin nature in its relentless pursuit to justify itself.

But Jesus said, "If you love Me, you will keep My commandments."[30] Notice it's love for Christ that motivates obedience to Him, not vice versa. And our love for Christ is directly proportionate to our understanding of His truth and the gratitude and affection that knowledge properly produces. We must therefore avoid this doctrinal and spiritual error at all costs lest we fall into the same trap as those in the world.

TOLERANCE AND THE TAIL END OF HISTORY

So how does this phenomenon of tolerance play into last-days apostasy? From what we've seen, today's tolerance is not simply a weakening of truth or values but rather a deliberate denial of them. The effects of this spiritual delusion are a part of the ear-tickling, end-times "myths" about which Paul solemnly warned Timothy. And Satan, who is both the god of this world and the prince of the power of the air, is he who fuels the grand illusion. Consistent with his nature, he lives up to his reputation as a liar, and the father of lies.[31]

Thankfully for us, though God does not tolerate sin, He does have patience with sinners. This truth prompted Habakkuk to argue,

> Your eyes are too pure to look on evil;
> You cannot tolerate wrongdoing.
> Why then do you tolerate the treacherous?
> Why are you silent while the wicked swallow up those
>   more righteous than themselves?[32]

No doubt you've had the same sentiment as you observe the world around you. While you know God is intolerant of sin, it appears He still allows an awful lot of it to continue.[33] But that's another reason why knowing Scripture is so important. The Bible also says there is coming a time when God's patience will come to an end. Peter reminds us, "The Lord is not slow in keeping his promise, as some understand slowness. Instead he is patient with you, not wanting anyone to perish, but everyone to come to repentance."[34]

Paul echoes this in Romans 2:4-5, warning unbelievers not to take for granted God's "forbearance" (tolerance):

> Or do you show contempt for the riches of his kindness, forbearance and patience, not realizing that God's kindness is intended to lead you to repentance?
>
> But because of your stubbornness and your unrepentant heart, you are storing up wrath against yourself for the day of God's wrath, when his righteous judgment will be revealed (NIV).

Clearly God's patience and tolerance are like sisters with similar DNA. Out of His grace and mercy, He withheld judgment on sins previously committed.[35] Even today, not all sin is punished immediately, but that does not mean God will wait forever. His present patience and tolerance is not *for* but rather *with* sinners. As long as there is breath (that breath itself being a gracious gift from God), there is still time for repentance.[36]

But His tolerance and patience will one day give way to global wrath. This begins in the seven years of Tribulation, where the "wrath of the Lamb" and of His Father are poured out upon earth and its inhabitants. Interestingly enough, even those who suffer this wrath know where it comes from, as Revelation 6:15-17 prophesies:

Then the kings of the earth, the princes, the
generals, the rich, the mighty, and everyone else,
both slave and free, hid in caves and among the rocks
of the mountains. They called to the mountains and
the rocks, "Fall on us and hide us from the face of
him who sits on the throne and from the wrath of
the Lamb! For the great day of their wrath has come,
and who can withstand it?" (NIV)

The Day of the Lord will be a day of ferocious intolerance. How much better to turn to God's grace while it is still
freely offered?

By every indication, these and other "hijackings" will
occur up to, and beyond, Christ's return for His church at
the Rapture. Immoral values and behavior will continue to
be not only tolerated but promoted and celebrated, while
at the same time biblical standards and those who adhere
to them will be demonized. This will create growing ten-
sion for believers who desire to reach others for Christ but
find themselves hindered by the fact that they are viewed as
narrow minded, bigoted, unscientific, or homophobic. This
will likely contribute to an even greater marginalization of
the church in society. As Nero famously made the church a
convenient scapegoat for the burning of Rome, so our world
will increasingly vilify believers in the years to come. Do not
be surprised when Christians are treated with contempt and
seen as "holding back progress" or "keeping us in the dark
ages." We are slowly becoming society's outcasts.

But if it's any consolation, so was the first-century church.

So in one sense, the world will become more tolerant while at the same time turning more rigid and biased toward Christians and their Christ. And this is yet another reason to eagerly anticipate the imminent return of Jesus Christ, like those early believers did.

Because we are living in the last days, time is not our friend. That's one reason Paul urged the Ephesian Christians to "[make] the most of your time, because the days are evil."[37] This reality ignites our hearts and lives not with panic but with purposeful urgency. It keeps us on track, laser focused on the faith that has been faithfully passed on to us.[38] In the church, what unites people from diverse backgrounds, races, and experiences is not that we are simply *tolerant* of one another but that we are bound together by a common faith in Jesus Christ. This is the essence of fellowship.[39] The apostles laid the foundation of the church, with Jesus Christ as the chief cornerstone. We are His "living stones." And we have to keep building the body, especially as we "see the day drawing near."[40]

This therefore, is *your* time in God's story. You want a strong ending, not a whimpering finish. So will you be a discerning Christian, one who sees through the deceptive fog of our day? Will you be a last-days revolutionary who takes up the banner of Christ, no matter what it costs? Will you champion His truth, refusing to tolerate mediocrity in your own heart? Will you fight the good fight and finish your course?

Will you keep the faith?

CHAPTER 6

MORAL FREEFALL

An Avianca Airlines jet crashed in Spain in 1984. The investigation into the crash uncovered an alarming conversation on the black box cockpit recorder. A few minutes before the plane plowed into the side of a mountain, a commanding voice from the plane's automatic warning system repeatedly cautioned in English, "Pull up! Pull up!" Believing the device was malfunctioning, the irritated pilot said, "Shut up, Gringo!" and shut the system off. Within minutes, the plane slammed into the side of a mountain, killing everyone on board.[1]

Similar to the airplane's warning system, the Bible, God's instruction manual and warning system, is quoted and obeyed as long as it fits an agenda, tells people what they want to hear, and agrees with their decisions and direction in life. Yet when the Bible warns them to "Pull up!"—to stop some sinful behavior or belief—they don't want to hear it and want to shut it up. Tragically, the result is a spiritual death spiral—a moral freefall without a parachute. This is true of an individual, a family, a church, and a nation.

BEHAVIOR FOLLOWS BELIEF

I like the story of the two hunters who came upon a huge hole in the ground. One hunter said to the other, "I can't even see the bottom of that hole! How deep do you think it is?" The other replied, "I don't know. Let's throw something down and listen for how long it takes to hit bottom."

"I saw an old automobile transmission nearby," the first hunter said. "Let's throw that in and see." So they found the transmission, hauled it over, and tossed it down the hole. While they listened for the transmission to hit bottom, they heard a rustling behind them. Then they saw a goat crash through the brush, run up to the hole, and jump in headfirst.

They were puzzled by this, and while they tried to sort it all out, an old farmer walked up. "You didn't happen to see my goat, did you?" he asked.

The first hunter said, "Funny you should ask. We were just standing here a minute ago when a goat ran out of the bushes and jumped headfirst into the hole!"

The farmer replied, "That can't possibly be my goat. I had him chained to a transmission!"[2]

In the same way that the goat followed the transmission, behavior follows belief. What we believe inevitably pulls our behavior with it. A. W. Tozer says, "It would be impossible to overemphasize the importance of sound doctrine in the life of the Christian. Right thinking about all spiritual matters is imperative if we would have right living. As men do not gather grapes of thorns nor figs of thistles, so sound character does not grow out of unsound teaching."[3]

Doctrinal departure from the truth eventually makes its way into the lives of people. A person becomes what he or she believes. Wandering away from the truth of the gospel leads inevitably to moral apostasy as night follows day. From the other side, what we believe is displayed in how we behave. In the Bible, apostasy involves both wrong belief (doctrine) and wrong behavior (doing). One's creed determines one's conduct and ultimately one's character.[4]

LAST DAYS DEPARTURE

The key New Testament text on the moral freefall in the visible church of the last days is 2 Timothy 3:1-13. The beginning of this passage highlights nineteen terrible characteristics of apostasy in the last days:

> Realize this, that in the last days difficult times
> will come. For men will be lovers of self, lovers

of money, boastful, arrogant, revilers, disobedient to parents, ungrateful, unholy, unloving, irreconcilable, malicious gossips, without self-control, brutal, haters of good, treacherous, reckless, conceited, lovers of pleasure rather than lovers of God, holding to a form of godliness, although they have denied its power; Avoid such men as these.[5]

The Message paraphrase of 2 Timothy 3:1-13 is helpful here with its graphic description of the attributes of the last days' apostasy:

Don't be naive. There are difficult times ahead. As the end approaches, people are going to be self-absorbed, money-hungry, self-promoting, stuck-up, profane, contemptuous of parents, crude, coarse, dog-eat-dog, unbending, slanderers, impulsively wild, savage, cynical, treacherous, ruthless, bloated windbags, addicted to lust, and allergic to God. They'll make a show of religion, but behind the scenes they're animals. Stay clear of these people.

These are the kind of people who smooth-talk themselves into the homes of unstable and needy women and take advantage of them; women who, depressed by their sinfulness, take up with every new religious fad that calls itself "truth." They get exploited every time and never really learn. These men are like those old Egyptian frauds Jannes and Jambres, who challenged Moses. They were rejects from the faith, twisted in their thinking, defying truth itself. But nothing will come of these latest impostors. Everyone will see through them, just as people saw through that Egyptian hoax. . . .

Unscrupulous con men will continue to exploit the faith. They're as deceived as the people they lead astray. As long as they are out there, things can only get worse.

There are five important keys to understanding this passage. First, Paul tells Timothy and us to "realize this." To put it in our language, Paul is saying, "Mark this, underline it, highlight it, don't miss it." In other words, this message about apostasy in the last days is something we need to pay full attention to and lay hold of. These verses are like a divine warning label about the last days. When Paul wrote 2 Timothy, he was languishing in a Roman dungeon. His earthly demise was near. His time on earth was winding down. His final inspired words drip with a sense of urgency.

Second, in the New Testament, the phrase "last days" relates to the entire time period between the ascension of Christ and His return.[6] We often call this period of time the inter-advent age or the church age.

The word "times" in 2 Timothy 3:1 means "seasons." We could translate verse 1, "In the last days wild seasons will come." What Paul is saying in the context of 2 Timothy 3:1 is that during the last days—a period of now almost two thousand years—there will be shorter seasons, periods, or intervals that will be especially difficult, terrible times of apostasy or falling away.[7]

The word "difficult" (*chelepoi*) in 2 Timothy 3:1 connotes the idea of "grievous" or "terrible." The only other place this Greek word is found in the New Testament is Matthew 8:28, where the two demoniacs were so *chelepoi* ("violent" or "wild") that no one could pass by. Plutarch used this word to describe "an ugly, infected, and dangerous wound."[8]

Putting all this together, Paul is telling us that the last days won't be uniformly evil but will be punctuated by repetitive cycles of ugly, dangerous, wild times. We're living in those uncontrollable times now.

Third, this passage says that while there will be seasons or times of apostasy that are especially terrible within the last days, the overall progression will be for things to worsen. We are told in verse 13 to expect apostasy to get worse as the church age progresses: "Evil men and imposters will proceed from bad to worse, deceiving and being deceived." In other words, as this extended period of time known as the last days unfolds, these perilous, uncontrollable times of apostasy will become more frequent and more intense as the return of Christ nears.

Fourth, we need to recognize that the conditions or symptoms described in 2 Timothy 3:1-13 are conditions *within* the visible church. Obviously, the kinds of sins listed here have always been prevalent in society at large. That's nothing new. The shocking thing here is that the sins of the culture become the sins of the church. Professing Christians are pictured living on the lowest level. The entire context of 2 Timothy 3 is describing people who profess to know God and hold to a form of godliness yet deny its power. Paul says clearly that there will be no lack of religion but that people will deny its power to transform the lives of people and society. As Ray Stedman says, "Paul tells us that the primary cause of these repetitive cycles of stress and danger is the hypocritical lives of people who profess to be Christians. They outwardly seem pious and religious but inwardly do not have the power of God in their lives. . . . When our light dims, the whole world sinks deeper into darkness."[9]

Don Carson states, "This appearance of godliness can have many different shapes. It may be fine liturgy or it may be a lot of exuberant noise. It may bubble over in a lot of fluent God-talk. What is missing, however, is the transforming power of the gospel that actually changes the lives of people."[10]

Fifth, the chief sin of the last days' apostasy, the one that heads the list, is that "men will be lovers of self." That's the real focus this list points to. Self-love is the polluted fountain from which the other eighteen characteristics flow. It is followed by "lovers of money" and then later comes "lovers of pleasure rather than lovers of God." (Notice it's not "lovers of pleasure *more* than God" but "*instead of* God." Love of God is replaced by love of pleasure.)

The present moral insanity and apostasy we're witnessing signals a radical shift from reverence for God to love of self.

In the last days, a kind of reverse Copernican revolution is occurring. The center of all existence is self instead of God, creating a black hole of depravity, where all kinds of sins and rebellion brew:

> The real problem with this vortex of ungodliness is that those who profess to be the people of God will be the ones displaying these characteristics. . . . They will give lip-service but not life-service. . . . They will have a form, but will deny the power that form would indicate they have. . . . In the last days religion will prosper, but so will wickedness, because what will pass for religion won't have any dynamite in it. Holding to a form of religion but denying its dynamite.[11]

Therefore, what we learn from this passage is that during the last days there will be times of especially serious, terrible, ugly moral apostasy in the visible church and that the overall trend and trajectory will be for the decadence and departure within the professing church to grow progressively worse.

LEANING LIVES

On a children's news TV show several years back, one of the segments reported that Italy's Leaning Tower of Pisa could possibly collapse, and to foster interaction with the audience, the reporters asked children to submit their solutions to the problem.

Several of the audience's fixes were featured, including a cable to haul the tower back, refrigeration coils to freeze the tower in place, and building adjacent to the tower to support the structure unobtrusively. But the most perceptive idea was a young boy's suggestion to "just build the buildings around it the same way and nobody will notice."

Many professing Christians today are adopting the same solution when it comes to the leaning world we live in. Rather than living godly lives as a witness to the crooked world, they build their lives on a slant so as not to attract any negative attention.[12]

The lowered standards within many churches and denominations are barely distinguishable from the world's. This reminds me of a story Philip DeCourcy shares about country music legend Willie Nelson, who bought a golf course. Someone once asked Willie what par was on the course. He answered, "Anything I want it to be. See that hole over there? It is a par 47." He added wryly, "And yesterday, I birdied it."[13] This is a funny story, but what isn't funny is that many within the church today regard morality the same way, lowering the behavioral bar so they can easily reach it. DeCourcy goes on to say,

> It seems that an increasing number of people don't believe in fixed or universal axioms of moral behavior. Right and wrong is determined by whatever the situation requires or whatever they believe is in their best interest. Ours is a day not

111

unlike the time of the Judges when, because there was no king in Israel every man did what was right in his own eyes (Judges 21:25). Ours is also a day not unlike that of the prophet Isaiah when men call evil good, and good evil (Isa. 5:20). Our increasingly secular society is rewriting the rules on morality (Judges 2:10). In a postmodern world there is no king or kingdom that rules over all, "all the ways of man are pure in his own eyes" (Prov. 16:2, 25; 21:2; 30:12). Each man is a law unto himself, and each social group its own kingdom. Man is autonomous, and free to indulge his sexual desires, decide his gender, live his life, and even end his life as he sees fit. This is the brave new world of ethics![14]

And this brave new world has invaded the church. We see it in the divorce rates within evangelical churches that are no different, and in some cases are even higher, than those of non-Christians. Lowered standards are also apparent in the prevalence of premarital sex and cohabitation among young adults who profess to be Christians, as well as pornography viewing among believers. In many vital areas, the church is not much different from the world.

THE ONLY OPINION THAT COUNTS

Moral apostasy, metastasizing out of the cancer of doctrinal apostasy, will escalate as the church age progresses, reaching its zenith just before Christ returns to catch to heaven all who have humbly accepted His Son as their Savior from sin.[15] The escalation of apostasy during this age is setting the stage for the final, ultimate apostasy that will occur under the Antichrist just before Christ returns to earth.[16]

In the meantime, as we await our Lord's return, our calling is to study and obey God's Word.

Umpire Babe Pinelli once called Babe Ruth out on strikes. When the crowd booed, Ruth challenged the umpire. "There's 40,000 people here who know that last pitch was a ball." The witnessing coaches and players prepared for Ruth to be ejected from the game. But Pinelli had a cool head and simply replied, "Maybe so, Babe, but mine is the only opinion that counts."

The church today needs to remember that when it comes to doctrine and morality, the only opinion that counts is God's. Second Timothy 3:14-17 makes this clear. Scripture is made up of the very words of God Himself. A chapter that opens under the ominous cloud of apostasy closes under the pure sunlight of the God-breathed Scriptures. God's Word is set forth as the answer to apostasy:

> But as for you, continue in what you have learned
> and have firmly believed, knowing from whom
> you learned it and how from childhood you have
> been acquainted with the sacred writings, which
> are able to make you wise for salvation through
> faith in Christ Jesus. All Scripture is breathed out

by God and profitable for teaching, for reproof, for correction, and for training in righteousness, that the man of God may be complete, equipped for every good work.[17]

Second Timothy 3:14 begins with the two little words—"but . . . you" (*su de* in Greek). In some ways, these are the key words in 2 Timothy. Four times Timothy is called to stand apart from what's happening around him.[18] He was the opposite of many contemporary Christians who have decided to *fit in* rather than *stand out*. He was faithful to learn and live out God's Word in his life.

God's Word is our source for detecting and rejecting apostasy.[19] Philip Ryken, the president of Wheaton College, writes that "according to tradition, coal miners would take a canary with them underground for safety. Canaries are fragile birds, and thus they are the first to suffer the harmful effects of unhealthy air. In the event of a lack of oxygen or a sudden influx of noxious gas, the canary would pass out and the miners would know that they needed to return to the surface."[20] Today, in the same way, God's Word is alerting us to the toxicity of the surrounding moral atmosphere. The Bible is like the canary down the mine shaft warning us of the deadly fumes seeping into the church. But the Bible is also the clear air that's the answer to the church's polluted environment.

Hearing and humbly obeying its call in our own lives to "pull up" is the only answer to our moral freefall.

CHAPTER 7

THE WATERSHED MOMENT
FOR THE CHURCH

JUNE 26, 2015, WAS A WATERSHED MOMENT in American history. The United States Supreme Court, in a case known as *Obergefell v. Hodges*, held that "the right to marry is a fundamental right inherent in the liberty of the person, and under the Due Process and Equal Protection Clauses of the Fourteenth Amendment couples of the same-sex may not be deprived of that right and that liberty."[1] The ruling further prohibits any state from hindering the marriage of same-sex couples and abrogates all statutes and state constitutional provisions that define marriage as the union of a man and a woman.

This ruling dealt a devastating blow to those who believe the Bible and its definition of marriage as a monogamous, heterosexual union and to all who hold the traditional view of marriage that has been recognized from time immemorial. With one stroke, natural marriage was no longer the exclusive definition of marriage in America. As saddening as the ruling is, it is not surprising to anyone who has followed the cultural trajectory of this issue. It was just a matter of time since the onset of the sexual revolution of the 1960s.

Nevertheless, what has been even worse than the US Supreme Court decision, if that's possible, is the response of many professing Christians, even Christian leaders, to this issue. In many quarters of professing Christianity the decision was met with acceptance, approval, and even applause, so much so that many mainline denominations and progressive "Christians" beat the Supreme Court to the punch.

A year before the *Obergefell* decision, the Presbyterian Church (USA) approved homosexual marriage. "The top legislative body of the Presbyterian Church (U.S.A.) voted by large margins . . . to recognize same-sex marriage as Christian in the church constitution, adding language that marriage can be the union of 'two people,' not just 'a man and a woman.'"[2]

About two weeks before the Supreme Court's decision, Tony Campolo, a well-known, outspoken Christian leader, came out in favor of gay marriage. Campolo's rationale was explained in CBN News:

> It was [Campolo's] own relationship with his wife and the many same-sex couples they know and spend time with that persuaded him that the primary purpose

of marriage is about spiritual growth. He also wrote that homosexuality is "almost never a choice" and the church should offer love and acceptance to those who have same-sex attraction. "It has taken countless hours of prayer, study, conversation and emotional turmoil to bring me to the place where I am finally ready to call for the full acceptance of Christian gay couples into the Church."[3]

Rob Bell, former pastor of Mars Hill Church, and his wife, Kristen, appeared with Oprah Winfrey on her *Super Soul Sunday* program. When asked about the church embracing same-sex marriage, Rob Bell said, "We're moments away. I think the culture is already there. And the church will continue to be even more irrelevant when it quotes letters from 2,000 years ago as their best defense."[4] His total discounting of Scripture is stunning.

Influential author and blogger Rachel Held Evans, who no longer considers herself an evangelical, offers full support for same-sex marriage, basing her position almost exclusively on feelings and a desire to affirm others rather than Scripture. She says, "As I've made it clear in the past, I support marriage equality and affirm my gay and lesbian friends who want to commit themselves to another person for life."[5] Many more similar, equally shocking quotes could be added to these. The blogosphere is filled with sympathetic endorsements by professing Christians who support homosexual relationships in the name of love and acceptance.[6]

Simply stated, the tide on this issue has turned in our culture, especially with those under age fifty and overwhelmingly with those under age thirty. For believers who have lived in America over the last few decades, our heads are still spinning. What on earth has just happened? How did we get here? While many factors contribute to a shift like this, three stand out.

First, behind this shift is a well-organized satanic strategy. The home is the foundation of society—the first human institution created by God. The main New Testament passage on spiritual warfare is Ephesians 6:10-18, which follows on the heels of a passage about marriage and the family. Satan is the avowed enemy of traditional, natural marriage and the home. There's no doubt that changing views on homosexual behavior—one of the defining issues of our time—is Satan's overt strategy to pervert, repurpose, and reinvent human identity. The devil's end game is to deceive and destroy every trace of conscience found in humanity, God's crown of creation. Satan is working to pry people away from the truth in every form—doctrinal and moral.

As the coming of Christ draws near, we should expect the enemy to step up his assault on the truth to prepare the world for the final great falling away predicted in 2 Thessalonians 2:2-3. The stunning pace with which homosexual behavior has gained approval can only be explained in supernatural terms. Something beyond human forces is energizing this issue and galvanizing the marginalization and mocking of those who disagree.

Second, the Bible and sound biblical teaching are fast

becoming relics. The Bible today is not faithfully taught in a growing number of churches. Confidence in God's Word as inspired and inerrant is eroding dramatically. People don't know what the Bible says, or don't care, or selectively believe what they want. Everything has become squishy and uncertain. With no final authority, the demise of a Christian worldview is upon us, and morality is a moving target subject only to the currents of culture. Christian Smith laments this trend from objective truth to subjective feelings: "While the vast majority of US teenagers identified themselves as Christians, the 'language,' and therefore experience, of Trinity, holiness, sin, grace, justification, sanctification, church, Eucharist, and heaven and hell appear, among most Christian teenagers in the United States at the very least, to be supplanted by the language of happiness, niceness and earned heavenly reward."[7] Smith and his colleagues call this new faith "Moralistic Therapeutic Deism," a belief system that embraces the existence of a god who demands little more than to be nice, "with the central goal of life to be happy and feel good about oneself."[8] In the prevailing climate of moralism and relativism, even within churches, we should not be surprised at what's happening.

Third, many professing believers are gripped by compromise and cowardice. In a society that increasingly delights in same-sex relationships and demonizes those who disagree, many are not willing to stand and face the fire. It's easier to cave and cower. Expect more and more professing Christians to take the path of least resistance and to just stay quiet or surrender to the waves of compromise and tolerance.

Nevertheless, the calling on God's people is to hold fast to Scripture and to love others, even in the face of being mocked and maligned for our convictions regarding this important issue.[9] True love for others involves graciously telling them the truth.

MORAL APOSTASY

Some might ask why we are highlighting homosexual behavior as a watershed for apostasy among the other sins in our culture. There are all kinds of sins out there, so why are we dedicating a chapter to this one? Are we just picking on this sin because it's an easy target? While we can't speak for all Christians, we believe there are three main reasons why homosexual behavior is a watershed issue related to apostasy.

First, in a unique way, this sin is contrary to nature and rubs against the grain of God's created order. Three times in Romans 1 Paul emphasizes that homosexual sin is contrary to nature or unnatural.[10] With this sin, a line is crossed that is different from other sins. A divinely appointed barrier is breached. Romans 1:27 seems to make that clear: "In the same way also the men abandoned the natural function of the woman and burned in their desire toward one another, men with men committing indecent acts and receiving in their own persons the due penalty of their error." In this one verse homosexuality is called unnatural, indecent, error, and bringing a due penalty.

In an attempt to blunt this point, many today argue that

all sins are the same. Homosexuality is no different from telling a lie, gossiping, or getting drunk, they argue, so why make such a big deal of it? Those who oppose the rapid acceptance of homosexual behavior are accused of overreacting on this issue and failing to maintain a sense of proportion. To be fair, this point is also often cited by those who are against homosexual behavior in an effort to be evenhanded. After all, all of us are sinners—and we say "amen" to that. But is that the end of the matter? Are all sins really the same?

The answer to this question is yes and no. Yes, all sins are the same in that they break God's law. They make the offender a lawbreaker.[11] They put the transgressor at odds with the law. In that sense all sins are the same. But no, all sins aren't the same in their effect and consequences. Any reading of the Old Testament law codes reveals a vast difference in punishment for various offenses. Differing punishment reveals that some sins are more serious than others.

The same thing is true in legal statutes today. Few would argue that traffic offenses are no different from rape, bank robbery, or kidnapping. Yes, all offenses break the law. All violations make you a lawbreaker. But no, not all have anywhere near the same consequences or call forth the same punishment. In Scripture, homosexuality is not treated like other sins.[12]

If someone shoots at a large plate-glass window with a BB gun, the BB breaks the glass. A small hole is made. The BB-shooting perpetrator is a glass breaker. If another person shoots a large plate-glass window with a bazooka, the bazooka shell shatters the glass. The bazooka-wielding perpetrator is also a glass breaker. But in this latter case, the glass is obliterated. It is not a tiny hole that is left behind but a colossal cavity. The window and all the structure around it are blown away. Both parties are glass breakers, and in this sense their acts are the same, yet who would argue that these acts are equal? Certainly not the owner of the window. The nature of these acts is vastly different. Consequences matter. Punishments are tailored to meet the extent of the damage inflicted. So when someone says all sins are the same to God, we need to make sure we accurately frame the issue.

The second reason homosexual behavior is a watershed issue for culture and the church—a bright red line—is that until very recently, belief that homosexual behavior is wrong was pervasive. Growing up in the '60s and '70s, people of all ages and walks of life considered same-sex physical intimacy wrong. Almost no one, including even the most hardened unbelievers, considered homosexual behavior acceptable. The avalanche in the last twenty years that has culminated in the nationwide legality of same-sex marriage has been nothing short of breathtaking. The radical redefining of marriage goes to the heart of humanity and society. The first human institution God created was marriage. Changing its definition means that nothing is sacred—nothing is off limits. Everything is up for grabs.

Third, more and more professing Christians are capitulating to the culture and accepting same-sex relationships. According to research conducted by the Pew Research Center, "the divide between evangelicals and mainline Protestants over gay marriage is getting wider. The survey found that 70 percent of white evangelicals and 57 percent of black Protestants don't support making same-sex marriage legal [that means one-third of white evangelicals and nearly one-half of black Protestants support it]. However, 62 percent of white mainline Protestants and 56 percent of Catholics are in favor of same-sex marriage."[13] The surrender of so many on this issue sounds the alarm for a reasoned response, a call to biblical discernment, and an answer to the question, How do we hold fast to Scripture and love all people, all the while being hated and demonized by the world for simply believing the Bible?

BACK TO THE BIBLE

For two thousand years the church of Jesus Christ has believed that homosexual behavior is sinful. Having a same-sex orientation is not sinful in itself, but acting on that orientation is contrary to Scripture. The distinction between having a same-sex orientation and acting on that desire is important, and we need to keep this point clearly before us.

Belief that homosexual activity is wrong was almost universally accepted even two or three decades ago among Christians and non-Christians alike. Stating the matter as simply as possible, Christians have believed, "God intended humans to express their sexuality within the confines of a marriage between a man and a woman only, not with someone of the same gender."[14]

Then, suddenly, when activists began to turn the tide of

public opinion, progressives in the church had an epiphany that homosexual behavior is acceptable to God. In a lemminglike rush, many could hardly give their blessing fast enough. But could it be that the change in position was borne not of *epiphany* but rather *expediency*—a desire to be embraced and accepted by the secular culture? Is the retreat rising from a desire to avoid the label of homophobia and to appear more loving and tolerant than believers who hold to the millennia-long interpretation of God's Word?

Turning to God's Word, there are four main biblical passages (or groupings) that refer negatively to the issue of homosexual activity:

1. The story of Sodom (Genesis 19:1-13)
2. The Levitical texts (Leviticus 18:22; 20:13)
3. Paul's description of fallen society away from God (Romans 1:26-32)
4. Two lists by Paul, each containing a reference to homosexual practice of some kind (1 Corinthians 6:9-10 and 1 Timothy 1:8-11)[15]

Let's look very briefly at each of these. (The Leviticus passages will be discussed in connection with 1 Corinthians 6.)

Genesis 19:1-13

The famous passage in Genesis 19 refers to the homosexual desires of the men of Sodom toward the two male visitors to their city—who were angelic beings in human form—and God's cataclysmic judgment of the city. Since that time, Sodom has become equated with divine judgment. John Stott writes, "To be sure, homosexual behavior was not Sodom's only sin; but according to Scripture it was certainly one of its sins, which brought down upon it the fearful judgment of God."[16] The Epistle of Jude confirms the link between Sodom's sexual sin and its destruction.[17]

Romans 1:26-32

Romans 1:26-27 says, "God gave them over to degrading passions; for their women exchanged the natural function for that which is unnatural, and in the same way also the men abandoned the natural function of the woman and burned in their desire toward one another, men with men committing indecent acts and receiving in their own persons the due penalty of their error."

While much could be—and has been—said about these verses, there's no doubt that the other activities listed in Romans 1:28-31 are sinful, and Romans 1:28-31 immediately follows the verses dealing with homosexuality. In this context, which catalogs serious sins, arguing that Paul didn't consider homosexual behavior to be a sin is quite a stretch. Kevin DeYoung says it well:

> Homosexual practice is sinful because it violates the divine design in creation. According to Paul's logic, men and women who engage in same-sex sexual

behavior—even if they are being true to their own feelings and desires—have suppressed God's truth in unrighteousness. They have exchanged the fittedness of male-female relations for those that are contrary to nature.[18]

1 Corinthians 6:9-10

First Corinthians 6:9-10 is an ugly list of sins that are incompatible and irreconcilable with the Kingdom of God and the gospel: "Or do you not know that the unrighteous will not inherit the kingdom of God? Do not be deceived; neither fornicators, nor idolaters, nor adulterers, nor *effeminate*, nor *homosexuals*, nor thieves, nor the covetous, nor drunkards, nor revilers, nor swindlers, will inherit the kingdom of God" (emphasis added).

Don't overlook the serious words of warning: "Do not be deceived." Many today, in failing to take these words seriously, *are* being deceived.

Two of the words used in these verses refer to homosexual behavior:

- *Malakos*, sometimes translated "effeminate," means "soft to the touch." Among the Greeks it referred to males who assumed the passive role in homosexual intercourse.
- *Arsenokoitai*, found in 1 Corinthians 6:9, is a compound of *arsen* (man) and *koite* (bed). An accurate translation is "bedder of man," or someone who takes men to bed. The clear meaning of the

word is men engaged in homosexual behavior. Paul probably referred back to Leviticus 18:22 and 20:13 in coining this word.[19] The Levitical passages call for the death penalty for homosexual intercourse and call it an "abomination." The related words in Romans 1:27, *arsenes en arsesin* ("men in men"), are a vivid, graphic reference to male homosexuals' intimacy.

Kevin DeYoung highlights the seriousness of these verses:

> If 1 Corinthians 6 is right, it's not an overstatement to say that solemnizing same-sex sexual behavior— like supporting any form of sexual immorality— runs the risk of leading people to hell. . . . When we tolerate the doctrine which affirms homosexual behavior, we are tolerating a doctrine which leads people further from God. This is not the mission Jesus gave his disciples when he told them to teach the nations everything he commanded.[20]

1 Timothy 1:8-10

Another vice list that condemns homosexual behavior is found in 1 Timothy 1:8-10:

> We know that the Law is good, if one uses it lawfully, realizing the fact that law is not made for a righteous person, but for those who are lawless and rebellious, for the ungodly and sinners, for the

unholy and profane, for those who kill their fathers or mothers, for murderers and immoral men and homosexuals and kidnappers and liars and perjurers, and whatever else is contrary to sound teaching.

Paul uses the word *arsenokoitai* in 1:10 (the same word used in 1 Corinthians 6:9) and clearly links this behavior with other sinful activities that are contrary to God's law.

To Believe or Not to Believe

Added to these texts, the biblical view of marriage set forth in Genesis 1–2 excludes homosexual acts by implication even if it never specifically prohibits them.[21] The positive principles in Genesis 1–2 and the consistent prohibitions of sexual immorality in the Old and New Testaments confirm monogamous, heterosexual marriage as the only one-flesh relationship God accepts and blesses. Scripture is very clear on this issue in spite of all the noise we hear today. Those who claim there is no unanimity on this issue among scholars must remember that until very recently there was. Just because people in recent days, influenced by cultural trends, have begun to question the long-standing interpretation of key passages does not mean the issue is foggy.

The question is, Do we believe the Bible is God's inspired Word, and are we willing to take what it says at face value, using accepted principles of interpretation? That the Bible prohibits homosexual behavior is clear cut to any objective interpreter. Those trying to twist Scripture to support homosexual behavior, or at least to muddy the waters, have utterly failed to make their case from Scripture.

Summarizing the New Testament prohibitions, Peter Coleman notes, "St. Paul's writings repudiate homosexual behavior as a vice of the Gentiles in Romans, as a bar to the Kingdom of God in Corinthians, and as an offense to be repudiated by the moral law in 1 Timothy."[22] Rod Dreher encourages young people and progressive Christians to hit the pause button on this issue:

> Homosexuality is a clear, bright line. The Rachel Held Evanses need to ask themselves if they would be willing to follow Jesus Christ if in doing so, they would have to take a countercultural position on the issue. To embrace same-sex marriage from a Christian viewpoint is a radical shift, one that repudiates two millenia of Christian thought and teaching.
>
> Are we really so sure that we 21st century Americans have this right, and everyone that came before us, including St. Paul, was wrong?[23]

These are sage words for us all to take to heart.

ARGUMENTS IN SUPPORT OF HOMOSEXUAL RELATIONS

Entire books have been written dealing with the arguments pro and con for homosexual behavior, so the purpose here is not to plumb the depths of this issue. In this section, however, we want to briefly state and answer a few of the most common contentions offered by proponents of homosexuality to support their view.

What's Love Got to Do with It?

One prevalent argument in favor of homosexual relationships is that love trumps all. If people love each other, what they do or who they do it with cannot be wrong. While this sounds appealing in our contemporary, tolerant culture, it is shortsighted. Love, which is an essential part of any intimate relationship, is not the sole criterion that authenticates it.[24] After all, what if a person loves several people? What if a person loves an animal? What if an adult loves a child and the child says he or she loves the adult? What if someone loves someone who is married to another person?

Love is found in obedience to the law and the purpose of our Creator, not in rebellion against it. As John Stott says, "No man is justified in breaking his marriage covenant with his wife on the ground that the quality of his love for another woman is richer. Quality of love is not the only yardstick by which to measure what is good and right. . . . There seems to be no limits to what some people will seek to justify in the name of love."[25] Love cannot be the sole criterion for sexual relationships. Love and law are not incompatible.[26]

Justice for All?

For many, the full acceptance of homosexual activity is a simple matter of justice and nondiscrimination. We often

hear about "gay rights," which implies homosexuals are suffering an injustice that needs to be righted. Desmond Tutu,
former archbishop of Cape Town, among many others,
pushes this point. But is this reasoning sound?

God is a God of justice and righteousness. He is infi-
nitely just, and He wants His creatures to love and respect
all people without distinction. However, it does not follow
that homosexual behavior should be condoned as a matter of
justice. Speaking about homosexuality and justice, John Stott
says, "Talk of 'justice' is inappropriate, since human beings
may not claim as a 'right' what God has not given them."[27]
Since the Creator has not given human beings the right to
express their sexuality with members of the same sex, any
talk of justice or rights on this topic is misplaced. People may
believe homosexual relationships are acceptable, but appealing to justice or rights to substantiate this position is contrary
to Scripture. "Sexual intimacy is legitimate, according to
Scripture, only within the confines of heterosexual marriage.
For this reason, homosexual practice cannot be regarded as a
permissible equivalent, let alone a divine right."[28]

Jesus Was Silent about Homosexuality

Some point to the fact that Jesus never condemned homosexuality as evidence of His implicit approval. There are
two problems with this notion. First, Jesus did not address
many sins. He never condemned child abuse, bank robbery,
or drug abuse, but certainly all of those activities are sinful.

Jesus never had to condemn homosexual behavior because everyone in the Jewish culture of His day understood that it was contrary to the Mosaic law.[29]

Second, Jesus frequently referenced Sodom (and a few times Gomorrah) to warn His listeners of impending doom.[30] The word *sodomy* comes from the homosexual sin of Sodom. Any argument that Jesus supported homosexuality is an argument from silence that disregards His numerous negative references to Sodom.

APPROVAL AND APPLAUSE

As we've seen, no fair-minded case can be made that Scripture supports homosexual acts or fails to condemn them. Homosexuals who fulfill their sexual desires are violating the will of their Creator. But the issue doesn't end there. The Bible not only prohibits same-sex relations but it also forbids approving or applauding this activity. In the same context in Romans 1 where Paul prohibits same-sex relations, he concludes, "Although they know the ordinance of God, that those who practice such things are worthy of death, they not only do the same, but also give hearty approval to those who practice them."[31]

Today, the cheering section for same-sex relationships and even homosexual marriage is mushrooming in our culture and within the church. Acceptance has given way to approval, which has in turn led to applause. This viewpoint has grown to such an extent that those who voice any objection are increasingly ostracized, maligned, and muzzled. Scores of pastors, church leaders, and denominations across the country lend hearty approval to what's happening in our culture and heap disdain on any who disagree. Evil is called good while good is called evil.

Romans 1:32 is a sobering warning against this attitude. Approving and applauding the sins listed in the preceding context (including same-sex relations) is harshly condemned by God. Romans 1:32 actually says that commending these sins is *worse* than committing them. How can that possibly be? Thomas Schreiner explains: "The person who commits evil, even though his or her actions are inexcusable, can at least plead the mitigating circumstances of the passion of the moment. Those who encourage others to practice evil do so from a settled and impassioned conviction."[32]

C. E. B. Cranfield, the eminent New Testament scholar, says, "There is also the fact that those who condone and applaud the vicious actions of others are actually making a deliberate contribution to the setting up of a public opinion favourable to vice, and so to the corruption of an indefinite number of other people."[33] When people "[take] delight in the sinfulness of others . . . wickedness has sunk to its lowest level."[34]

What we're witnessing today is the graphic fulfillment of this principle. The applause is drowning out the voice of disagreement. According to Romans 1:32, those who are applauding the Supreme Court decision legalizing same-sex marriage are practicing an evil graver than those who are guilty of homosexual sin. That's sobering. It's the bottom rung on the ladder. When this point is reached to the extent we see today, the final falling away predicted in Scripture could certainly be just around the corner.

FINAL APOSTASY

The homosexual revolution has hit like a flood in the last twenty years. A red line has been crossed that few believed possible. In the wake of this departure, culture has already absorbed and accepted this behavior and moved past it to every form of gender confusion one can imagine. Nothing seems off limits or taboo. Every person does what is right in their own eyes. Issues of gender and identity are the new hot topic. In a recent article, ABC News identified fifty-eight genders for Facebook users to choose from.[35] Some have identified more than eighty different gender identifications. The question is being raised, Have we reached the end of gender? Many websites have eliminated any request for gender because they can't list them all or aren't sure how many to list. We even have gender-neutral translations of the Bible. Homosexuality was only the beginning—the opening volley. Having lost God, man has now lost himself. Where's it all headed?

Jesus said the world in the days before His second coming will be like the days of Lot in the city of Sodom:

> It was the same as happened in the days of Lot: they were eating, they were drinking, they were buying,

they were selling, they were planting, they were building; but on the day that Lot went out from Sodom it rained fire and brimstone from heaven and destroyed them all. It will be just the same on the day that the Son of Man is revealed.[36]

What is happening today is no coincidence or happenstance. Satan is spearheading a global onslaught against God and man to pave the way for the final apostasy predicted in 2 Thessalonians 2:2-3. We are living on its leading edge. This may be the beginning of the end.

Christ's coming may be very soon!

HIS WORD, THE LAST WORD

Same-sex issues—one single controversial reality—is having a profound effect on the church and individual Christians who don't know either what to believe or how they should respond biblically. We've seen in this chapter that we cannot approve what God disapproves. The church of Jesus Christ is a place for all of us to learn to say no to sin and to find spiritual help to live a life that pleases God. Every believer must take up the cross, dying to self and following Jesus regardless of our specific entangling sins. Our choice today on this issue is not between lazily condoning sinful behavior or lashing out in anger and condemnation. "There's another way. It's possible to show love and also speak of transformative truth. It just isn't easy."[37]

As Satan mounts his final, furious assault against the truth and seeks to erase every vestige of morality, we can rest humbly in the knowledge that God honors those who rely upon Him, submit to His will, and seek to lovingly encourage others to do the same.

Dawson Trotman, founder of the Navigators, used four code letters to refer to his nightly study of God's Word: HWLW. Whenever he was home with his wife or with a group of people at night and the conversation was waning, he would end with "HWLW"—"His Word the Last Word." One of them would recite a portion of Scripture, and they would head to bed. Trotman developed this practice as a way to keep the last thoughts of his day fixed on the Lord.

That's a great practice for ending the day, but it's an equally effective way to face the issues of our day. In every issue of life, our attitude should be HWLW—"His Word the Last Word."

May the Word of God have the Last Word in our lives, our families, our nation, and in His church as we await His coming.

CHAPTER 8

WILL THE REAL JESUS STAND UP?

[Jesus] said to them, "But who do you say that I am?"

MATTHEW 16:15

JESUS CHRIST IS THE MOST PIVOTAL, revolutionary, and controversial figure in human history. Concerning this, there is no debate. This one man accomplished more in His short life than kings and empires have done over centuries. And though the world's libraries are filled with volumes written about Him and His impact on humanity, one familiar work has become a classic. In his memorable poem "One Solitary Life," Dr. James Allan Francis describes Jesus' humble beginnings and ignominious death. But he goes on to describe Jesus' matchless influence:

Nineteen centuries have come and gone
And today Jesus is the central figure of the human race
And the leader of mankind's progress
All the armies that have ever marched
All the navies that have ever sailed
All the parliaments that have ever sat
All the kings that ever reigned put together
Have not affected the life of mankind on earth
As powerfully as that one solitary life.[1]

But despite Jesus' colossal impact on history and humanity, there exists today widespread confusion as to who He actually was . . . and is. There are, in fact, some who claim He never was at all.[2] And then there are those, like author Bart Ehrman, who assert that Jesus Himself never actually claimed to be deity; rather, His recorded claims were nothing more than a legend created by His followers after His death.[3]

But even among those who believe Jesus was God in the flesh, there are divergent views concerning His identity, mission, and accomplishments. Within Christendom exists a multiplicity of images floating around in the heads of those who profess to know Him. Therefore, history's refrain has become a recurring question confronting each new generation: Who *is* Jesus Christ? Or perhaps a more appropriate postmodern, theologically emerging question would be "Who is Jesus *to you?*"

Popular perception of Jesus is changing in culture and

even in the church. Scripture's Jesus is getting a makeover, and in some cases undergoing an *extreme* makeover. Take a survey of Main Street or a typical college campus, and you will likely find a surprising percentage of people haven't the slightest clue as to His real identity. I (Jeff) have done this in England, where young people's answers ranged from "I've no idea" to "Isn't he that bloke who did magic?"

Thanks to the overwhelming secularization in society, we're beginning to see a dramatic drop in the most basic biblical knowledge about Jesus. A recent Barna Group study revealed that fewer than 50 percent of millennials believe Jesus was God, and 56 percent of millennials either believe He was sinful like other humans or have confusion on the issue.[4]

But among those in America with a rudimentary knowledge of Christ, many have rejected long-held beliefs about the Son of God, favoring instead a reimagined version of Him. To them, He's due for an upgrade—Jesus 2.0, a new and improved Christ for a new generation. In an age of evolving spirituality, Jesus has come to mean anything you want Him to mean, really—a *customized* Savior for all peoples and preferences. A morphing Messiah.

JESUS VS. "JESUS"

Every new generation is responsible to engage and respond to God's revelation of Himself and His Son. However, in the absence of an understanding firmly anchored in Scripture, people's perceptions of Christ become skewed, blurred, and distorted. As a result, counterfeit Christs have appeared on the scene. And the values promoted in these various subdivisions of the Christian community give us insight into the "Christ idea" they follow. Here are a few you may recognize.

Hipster Jesus

Hipster Jesus is cool and very *chill*. After all, He has to be if we're going to reach a demographic of skinny-jeans-wearing, beard-growing, Pabst Blue Ribbon–drinking twentysome-things, right? Hipster Jesus is a handsome, handy, do-it-yourselfer. He's really into storytelling. In fact, *everything* is about story. He feeds the poor and gives handouts to the homeless. He stands up for human rights. In some circles, He may even have socialist leanings, since that's the way many in the younger generations view the early church. But though Hipster Jesus is big on diversity, His following is to a large degree white. And for some reason, Hipster Jesus doesn't go over that well in poor communities. This Jesus is very concerned about the environment and climate change. He wants His followers to be responsible stewards of the planet. He recycles and buys His clothes secondhand. He likes coffee shops and indie music. He prefers "worship arts pastors" to "ministers of music." He might be gluten free. He doesn't get too bent out of shape with specific doctrines or stress about whether pastors preach expository or topical sermons. He's more into *general* theology, if any at all. He sees value in returning to traditional liturgy.

Equality Jesus

This Jesus is much more liberal than Hipster Jesus, though in places there is some overlap. He isn't concerned about the "antiquated morality" fundamentalist Christians claim that Scripture teaches. So if certain Bible verses don't exactly square with our society's evolving beliefs or practices involving gender, sexuality, or marriage, this Jesus isn't going to get upset if you reinterpret or ignore them. Equality Jesus can't be accused of being on the wrong side of history. Those who subscribe to Equality Jesus say He is all about love and inclusion . . . as *they* define it, of course. His favorite word is *all*, and to His followers, phrases like "whosoever will come" and "just as I am" don't simply mean Jesus accepts you as you are; they mean He is perfectly okay with whoever you *want* to be. Those who believe in Equality Jesus not only redefine words like *love* and *hate* for a new age, but they also reclassify various sins, designating attitudes like bigotry and discrimination as among the most heinous, evil transgressions one could ever commit. Equality Jesus is a superhero social-justice warrior and will probably let everyone into heaven eventually. On the other hand, He may decide to keep out those pharisaical, bigoted, Bible-thumping conservatives.

Patriotic Jesus

This Jesus is the older counterpart to the one portrayed by the hipster crowd. Patriotic Jesus is ultraconservative, especially when it comes to moral issues. He leans far to the right in His politics, and His followers are expected to be heavily involved in the political process. There is no short supply of politically laced sermons in the Patriotic Jesus church culture. In fact, pastors routinely surrender their pulpits to like-minded politicians who happen to stop by. As a result, these politicians gain the "evangelical vote" when they campaign for "Judeo-Christian values" or moral issues that gain this particular religious or socioeconomic demographic's sympathy. Sometimes these voters ignore a personal lack of character in their chosen candidates because they're strong on the "right" issues.

Patriotic Jesus loves America and thinks it is the best nation He ever founded. It makes Him happy when His people fly the American flag in church and celebrate all the really important patriotic holidays. In that sense, this Jesus is very American. His followers talk about America being a "city on a hill" and a "light for all the nations." The United States is seen as sort of a new Israel or some kind of collective covenant people. There's talk about America being a "Christian nation," although Patriotic Jesus' followers sometimes struggle to articulate what that means. Patriotic Jesus supports the US military.

In many ways, Patriotic Jesus looks a lot more like a product of America than of heaven, much more earthly than eternal. He seems more concerned with temporal, national issues than He is with the destiny of people's souls. This Jesus is blatantly white and popular with middle- to upper-middle-class households.

Christ Caricatures

There are many other Christ caricatures in our culture that we could discuss, but they also fall far short of the Savior we see described in Scripture.

What makes these Christ caricatures compelling is that there are some elements of truth sprinkled into these interpretations of the incarnate Christ—truth easily ascertained from reading the Gospels. The Jesus of the Bible does care about social justice and those who are oppressed. On morality, He would be deeply offended and angered by sex trafficking, violence, and today's barbaric slaughter of innocent babies. And He does receive anyone who calls on His name for salvation. And when His people find themselves fortunate enough to be in a democracy, they can and should participate in the political process, especially when government promotes godless values and threatens religious liberty. The real Jesus suffered God's wrath to remove the penalty and power of sin for all sinners who trust in Him.

But despite what these aforementioned caricatures of Christ get right, they fail to provide the clarity and *totality* of who Jesus is as portrayed in Scripture. A *partial* Jesus is no Jesus at all. We cannot choose those parts of Him that appeal to us while ignoring the rest of who Scripture says He is. Christianity is not a biblical-truth buffet, where we hold our noses and pass over the items that fail our personal taste test. We do not set the menu of truth; God does.

Beyond trying desperately to relate Jesus to the next

generation, what we've witnessed in some church movements is a redefinition of the very essence of Jesus Himself. Is this a case of the church trying too hard? Loosely based on the Bible's Jesus, these caricatures of Him are like suffering through a bad movie that's "inspired by true events" or "based on the book." In such films, the depictions of characters often bear little or no resemblance to the actual persons they represent. Though some who promote these incomplete Christ caricatures may have honorable motives, by force fitting our Christ into our culture, we end up creating a "hybrid Jesus," one who may be more suited to today's changing world but is far away from the real Jesus known in Scripture. These images of Jesus may have some strengths, but their attempt to make Him more relevant than He already is proves to be a failed experiment. The portrait of Jesus that Scripture paints cannot be improved upon.

God needs no help with His theology, and He doesn't stutter when He speaks. Like Moses, we may protest His proclamations, but we cannot argue their veracity.

Altering or arguing the biblical concept of the Christ, even in the most minute way, blurs our vision of Him, quickly turning our incomplete, self-manufactured image of Him into an idol.

COMING INTO FOCUS

By detaching ourselves from Scripture's Jesus, we not only end up with the wrong Jesus, but we also short-circuit the very power of the gospel. Like the Father and the Spirit, remove any attributes of Jesus, and He suddenly becomes another Jesus altogether. Therefore, we do not need a "fresh vision" of Christ; we need a much more biblical one.

In His address to the seven churches in Revelation, Jesus reviews and repairs His distorted image by unmistakably presenting Himself with clarity and authority. There He describes Himself as a redeeming, loving, glorified, all-encompassing, sovereign, death-conquering, sword-wielding, judgment-bringing, Second Coming Lord and King![5] Is that how you see Him? Or is He still walking around in sandals, passing out fish and healing sick people? The vision of the resurrected, glorified Christ in Revelation is both terrific and traumatic, unbelievable and unforgettable. And it is only *after* imparting this vision that Jesus begins His extremely "tough love" rebuke of the churches. Hence, we can never become the Christians we were meant to be or properly understand our mission apart from a clear concept and understanding of who Jesus Christ is.

What would Jesus say to those churches today who are known not for proclaiming this Revelation Christ but rather for their happy messages, large crowds, and elaborate stage presentations? What would He say to congregations where there is much talk about *relationship* but little talk about *repentance*? There's celebration without sacrifice. A high value placed on friendship but not much emphasis on lordship. This is where the threat of apostasy is most subtle. Like a hairline fissure in a foundation, it's only the beginning of an eventual catastrophic collapse. Unless a contextually complete portrait of Jesus is taught, sung, believed, and celebrated, we end up missing the mark and getting the short stick of spirituality. God wants us to know and embrace *all* of His Son, not just the parts we prefer. We must see the big picture of Him, not conveniently chosen snapshots of His life, character, and ministry.

The good news is that it's not left up to us to define who God's Son is. God has already done the heavy lifting for us, providing us all we need to know through the revelation of Scripture. And that is to our advantage because our judgment can't be trusted anyway. Due to sin's effects on our minds and on our ability to comprehend spiritual truth, God did for us what we could never do for ourselves— He helped us discover what He is really like. During Jesus' earthly ministry, Jesus refused to trust people's hearts and intentions, even after some "believed in His name." John records that Jesus "was [still] not entrusting Himself to them, for He knew all men, and because He did not need anyone to testify concerning man, for He Himself knew what was in man."[6]

Jesus knows the true motives of people's hearts. And He understands that left to our own flawed imaginations, we'll usually get it wrong when describing, understanding, or explaining God. He knows we have a crippling disability when it comes to finding Him and understanding Him on our own. Our natural minds are darkened as it relates to comprehending His truth.[7] Even after coming to faith, we are still desperately dependent on the Holy Spirit's illuminating ministry, as we are prone to misinterpret and subtly twist God's Word.

But that's exactly why He gave us the Bible. As we engage it, the Author reveals His truth; our minds are opened to understand it. The Holy Spirit "turns on the lights," allowing us to see clearly and understand fully.[8]

Without God's divine revelation, we may end up believing in Him for all the wrong reasons. Or equally disastrous, the "Jesus" we choose to embrace may stem from a faulty, self-generated perception of who He actually is. One unintended result of this is that our expectations of Him can become unrealistic or unbiblical due to our own unbiblical understanding or conclusions. Instead of responding to and worshiping the Christ of Scripture, we would project an insufficient replica of Him onto our faith experience. We see this happening in these last days, not only as false Christs have appeared but also with the previously mentioned warped depictions of Him.[9]

As believers, we must guard against embracing a Savior who simply suits our spiritual taste buds or fits our theological, social, moral, and political constructs. Though it's human nature to do so, it becomes intrinsically defective and dysfunctional.

It's also sinful.

So one of the dangers of apostasy that we face right now is a "Jesus" who is both inaccurate and incomplete. Because many today have molded Him into whatever they want or need Him to be, He has become a "conjured-up Christ": loosely biblical but with all the practical details filled in by the human imagination. He is a god of our own making, a creation borne out of fantasy rather than reality. Tragically, failing to understand who Jesus is and what He came to accomplish leads to a false conclusion about the nature of the gospel itself. Emergent theologian Brian McLaren is one of those who paints an inaccurate portrait of Christ. In his book, *A New Kind of Christianity*, he writes,

> Instead, [Jesus] came to announce a new kingdom, a new way of life, a new way of peace that carried good news to all people of every religion. A new kingdom is much bigger than a new religion, and *in fact it has room for many religious traditions within it.* This good news wasn't simply about a new way to solve the religious problems of ontological fall and original sin (problems, remember once more, that arise centuries later and within a different narrative altogether). It wasn't simply information about how individual souls could leave earth, avoid hell, and ascend to heaven after death. No, it was about God's will being done on earth as in heaven for all people. It was about God's faithful solidarity with all humanity in our suffering, oppression, and evil.[10]

This redefining of Christianity is not a new understanding but simply an unbiblical one. McLaren's misunderstanding of Jesus and His substitutionary atonement makes it clear that in these last days, we need a passionate return to God and His Word in order to form and transform our understanding of His Son.

SO ... ANSWER THE QUESTION

One of the pleasant ironies of truth is that the sovereign, exalted Christ doesn't have a problem relating to mortals like us. On the contrary He identifies with all of humanity, including people from every race, tribe, tongue, and nation. He understands our struggles because He actually "became flesh, and dwelt among us."[11]

Hebrews reminds us,

> Since the children share in flesh and blood, He Himself likewise also partook of the same. . . . He had to be made like His brethren in all things, so that He might become a merciful and faithful high priest in things pertaining to God, to make propitiation for the sins of the people. For since He Himself was tempted in that which He has suffered, He is able to come to the aid of those who are tempted.[12]

And again, "We do not have a high priest who cannot sympathize with our weaknesses, but One who has been tempted in all things as we are, yet without sin."[13]

Jesus understands what it's like to walk the earth. Like us, He worked, sweat, grew hungry, and became tired. He felt the wide range of emotions we feel—joy and peace, along with sadness, disappointment, and the dark night of the soul. He experienced the hurt of being abandoned by those He loved the most, and He identifies with our mental stress and physical abuse. He bled and died. He was 100 percent human.

In fact, this was one of the reasons He came down from heaven and took on human flesh: to let us know that He really does get what it's like to be one of us. This is what qualifies Him to be a sympathetic Savior.[14]

But He also came to reveal the Father to us, to accomplish redemption, and to become our sin substitute. In doing so, He now represents us to the Father.[15] And though His identification with us doesn't allow us to perpetually morph Him into a fantasy of who we wish Him to be, it does tell us He *understands*.

The issue today isn't really, "Does Jesus get *us*?" but rather "Do we get *Him*?"

That's precisely the question the Lord asked His disciples toward the end of His earthly ministry: "Who do people say that the Son of Man is?" And after they reported what they had heard from the "social media" of their day, Jesus got more personal: "But who do *you* say that I am?"

Peter, the resident blurter of the Twelve, correctly responded, "You are the Christ, the Son of the living God."[16]

Good answer, Peter. You've been paying attention.

But Jesus didn't ask them this question so He could know how to more effectively relate to them or somehow accommodate their preferred image of Him. (These Jewish disciples expected the Christ to deliver them from Roman oppression and to set up His earthly kingdom in their lifetime.) Rather, He quizzed them so they could reveal whether or not they had developed an accurate and authentic concept of Him in their minds, to show whether or not *they* had received and processed the truth He had been teaching them. In forming their perception and understanding of Jesus Christ, it was imperative that they see the whole picture and not just the bits that accommodated their preconceived ideas. Their conclusion?

He was 100 percent God.

And He still is. There is, and will only ever be, one Jesus. He doesn't adapt, evolve, or change but is the same "yesterday and today and forever."[17] And His Word—not our emotional needs, cultural trends, church-growth fads, missional philosophies, or theological preferences—is our source of authority regarding Him.

Jesus is who Scripture says He is. Period. To augment that definitive biblical declaration is to create a "Frankenstein" god, pieced together with parts we've dug up and stitched together along our spiritual journey. Therefore, we dare not transform the Jesus who turned water to wine into a watered-down version of Himself. This is why we check every thought, belief, and teaching, sifting it through the filter of Scripture to see if it holds up as true. And if not, we reject it, no matter how attractive it may appear to be.

EXPERIENCING GOD

Fortunately, the Lord doesn't bypass our minds in order to reach our hearts. Even in the most basic, infantile decision to trust Christ, there must first be some existing knowledge of who that

Christ is and what He has done. Therefore, *experiencing* Jesus doesn't happen unless we first *know* something about Him. God designed and made us, intricately crafting humanity in body, mind, and spirit.[18] And He created us to respond to Him based on His revelation. Our experience of Him grows out of receiving and believing what He says is true about Himself. Any other experiential claim is unbiblical and heretical.

That's one reason Jesus, on His last night before being crucified, filled His high priestly prayer with language that was heavy on content and high on life change. Consider what He prayed for His disciples (and for you) in John 17:

- "That they may *know* You" (verse 3).
- "I have *manifested Your name* to the men whom You gave Me" (verse 6).
- "They have kept Your *word*" (verse 6).
- "The *words* which You gave Me *I have given* to them" (verse 8).
- "They *received them* [the words] and truly *understood* that I came forth from You" (verse 8).
- "These things I *speak in the world*, so that they may have *My joy made full*" (verse 13).
- "I have given them *Your word*" (verse 14).
- "*Sanctify them in the truth; Your word is truth*" (verse 17).
- "I have *made Your name known* to them . . . that the love with which You loved Me may be in them" (verse 26).

So even the joy and love we all long for begins with understanding and embracing God's revelation about Jesus! Apart from Scripture, we can know virtually nothing about Jesus Christ.[19]

So what do you believe about Jesus Christ? What's He like? What did He do? What theological truths did He teach? Further, what did He do for your sin? How can you know how to walk with Him daily? What do you need to know about God, the Christian life, Satan, the world, your sin nature, and how sanctification works? What do you do when you sin, and why don't you lose your salvation? *All* of these—and countless other topics—are a part of doctrine and theology. And they are all found within the pages of your own Bible.

You can rest in the confidence that yours is a God who is as holy as He is loving, as wrathful as He is gracious. The humble Jesus of the Gospels is the same exalted coming, conquering Christ of Revelation. The same Jesus who proclaimed, "Blessed are the poor in spirit" in Matthew 5:3 also prophesied in Matthew 7:23 concerning the day when He would say, "I never knew you; depart from Me, you who practice lawlessness." The same Jesus who beckoned, "Come to Me, all who are weary and heavy-laden, and I will give you rest" also predicted that some will "be cast into the outer darkness; in that place there will be weeping and gnashing of teeth."[20] The same Christ who comforts a grieving Mary and Martha in John 11 also offended thousands of followers in John 6. We cannot have one Jesus without the other.

He is all this and much more. He is one and the same—a complete Christ, not a cafeteria version of Himself.

Know that in these last days, there will be a continued assault on this biblical Jesus. As we are already seeing, He will be depicted as a Savior who winks at wickedness; who simply makes people feel good about themselves; who promises health, happiness, and prosperity; and who promotes tolerance and unity over discernment and doctrine. This makeshift Savior is heavy on sentimentality and light on sovereignty. Today's Jesus welcomes everyone into heaven regardless of religion. Some have made fantastical claims of visiting this heaven and have described Jesus Christ differently than Scripture does. And though millions swallow their syrupy tales and emotion-tugging lies, don't you be one of them.[21]

The lord of deception is a master at distorting the truth about the One who will one day cast him into the lake of fire.[22]

Many erroneous things will be said, preached, blogged, written, and sung about Jesus in the days to come. But we must hold fast to God's truth and not be swayed by false teachers and phony images of Christ. With Scripture as our anchor and rudder, we won't be "tossed and blown about by every wind of new teaching . . . [or] be influenced when people try to trick us with lies so clever they sound like the truth."[23]

Marry your mind and heart to God and His Word. And watch the Real Jesus stand *up* and stand *out* in your life.

CHAPTER 9

ACTS OF THE APOSTATES

Be on guard for yourselves and for all the flock.

ACTS 20:28

MEANDERING THROUGH THE BEAUTIFUL Welsh countryside
are endless arteries of narrow, hedgerow-lined lanes. These
tiny roads are so narrow it's a wonder two cars can pass
each other without colliding. While I (Jeff) was speaking
in England a few years ago, my host pastor took my wife
and me on a day trip into the Black Mountains of Wales.
Winding our way through the back roadways of that ancient
land, we crested a hill and came upon a shepherd herding his
sheep across our path. Coming to a stop, we rolled down our
windows to get a better look. The old farmer, outfitted with
a wooden staff, wellies, a tweed jacket, and a hat to match,
dutifully guided his flock across the rural lane.

Accompanied by a loyal border collie, the man glanced in our direction, then suddenly whistled, and the entire flock began scurrying across the road. He whistled again, this time with a slight variation, and the whole herd turned through a gate and into a fenced pasture, with the border collie assisting. I remember being amazed at how easy and effortless it all seemed. Just a whistle, the slightest sound from the man's mouth, and dozens of ewes, lambs, and rams obediently navigated their way to greener meadows.

One of the most picturesque ways Jesus describes Himself is as a shepherd. Once again he displays His brilliance in effective communication. Jesus' generation understood well the world of shepherds and sheep, as they were plentiful in His day and culture. And so, drawing upon that familiar way of life, the Lord beautifully illustrates the pastoral role He plays in our lives. After describing Himself as the "door of the sheep" (i.e., the only way to God), He continues, "I am the good shepherd; the good shepherd lays down his life for the sheep."[1] And later, "I am the good shepherd, and I know My own and My own know Me. . . . My sheep hear My voice, and I know them, and they follow Me."[2] But instead of whistling at His flock, our Lord personally "calls his own sheep *by name*, and leads them out."[3]

What a Savior!

This intimate connection Jesus has with us has so many facets to it, and all of them are for our benefit. As shepherd, He is Protector, even to the point of laying down His life for us, which He willingly did at the Cross.[4] But He is also our

Provider, leading us to still waters and rich, green pastures, giving us a life that, according to John 10:10, is truly *abundant* and satisfying. That is, in part, why He is the Good Shepherd. He desires only what is best for us because He knows us and loves us. Jesus Christ is the "Great Shepherd of the sheep."[5]

However, according to Scripture, we sheep have other shepherds as well—"undershepherds," if you will—those to whom God has entrusted the care of His people. We call them pastors.[6] A pastor (or elder) is one to whom a certain responsibility of oversight in the church is given. Implicit within that role and responsibility is a duty to preach and teach the Word of God. In fact, this is the primary way a pastor shepherds his flock, the church, which Paul describes as *the* "pillar and foundation of the truth."[7] In a fallen world, the church is what primarily upholds, supports, and defends God's revelation to mankind, and her godly presence and influence, via the indwelling Holy Spirit, are currently preventing a tidal wave of sin, depravity, and chaos from hitting earth's shores.[8] Being a pastor is a sobering responsibility, and those who are called to pastor must understand what an honorable yet serious task it is to lead God's people.

Paul reminded young pastor Timothy of both the gravity and necessity of this duty, urging the young minister to:

- Be "constantly nourished on the words of the faith and of the sound doctrine."[9]
- Make sure Scripture was read publicly to the church, along with "exhortation and teaching."[10]

- "Take pains with these things; be absorbed in them."[11]
- "Pay close attention to yourself and to your teaching."[12]

In his final letter to Timothy, Paul further strengthens his exhortation, writing,

> I solemnly urge you in the presence of God and Christ Jesus, who will someday judge the living and the dead when he comes to set up his Kingdom: Preach the word of God. Be prepared, whether the time is favorable or not. Patiently correct, rebuke, and encourage your people with good teaching.
>
> For a time is coming when people will no longer listen to sound and wholesome teaching. They will follow their own desires and will look for teachers who will tell them whatever their itching ears want to hear. They will reject the truth and chase after myths.
>
> But you should keep a clear mind in every situation. Don't be afraid of suffering for the Lord. Work at telling others the Good News, and fully carry out the ministry God has given you.[13]

Paul's words make it clear that you have to be crazy or called by God to be a pastor! Clearly the apostle believed the study, understanding, and communication of God's truth was to be a high priority in the church. And even more so considering the context of his earlier words: "But the Spirit explicitly says that *in later times* some will *fall away* from the faith, paying attention to deceitful spirits and doctrines of demons."[14] "Later times" here refers to the time between Christ's first coming and when he returns for His bride.[15] This time period is where we currently find ourselves.

And like other signs of the end times, this falling away will increase dramatically the closer we get to Revelation's day.[16] The Greek word translated "will fall away" is related to our word *apostasy*. And how does Paul say these people will desert the faith? By "paying attention to deceitful spirits and doctrines of demons." Satisfying self and luring humanity away from God and His truth have long been two of Satan's top strategies. He is known in Scripture as the one who "deceives the whole world" in the end times.[17] He is the "father of lies," the "god of this age," and the "ruler of demons," who themselves also rule over the darkness.[18]

Satan's deceptiveness is further seen in his ability to transform into an "angel of light," meaning he regularly masquerades as a messenger of truth. It is then no surprise that his servants impersonate "servants of righteousness." Paul says these messengers are, in reality, "false apostles" and "deceitful workers."[19] The men Paul writes about here desired the authority, respect, and influence that came with being an apostle of Christ, and they used self-made, artificial credentials to undermine Paul's ministry and mission. And while there are no living apostles today, this fact has in no way deterred Satan from his efforts to lead God's people astray through subtle, demonically inspired deception and doctrines. And even through some who claim to be "apostles."

THE NEW APOSTATES

But heretics don't fly into churches on brooms, maniacally mocking Scripture and terrorizing the flock. They don't show up sporting horns and sinister smiles. Rather, they gain entrance into the fold through persuasive words, self-help principles, and charismatic personalities. They enter via slick, well-designed websites and blogs, bringing promises of personal utopia for their followers. They are well groomed, attractive, smiling, likable, inspiring, convincing, and most of all *marketable*. Their mission is to make you happy; to make you feel good about yourself. They want to help you make the world a place of "Justice. Peace. Love. Equality."[20] Of course, each of those virtues is redefined to accommodate and conform to an ever-evolving worldly value system.[21] Their portrayal of Jesus' love is like a magic blanket that somehow mutes other, more disturbing attributes of God or uncomfortable truths found in the Bible.

Though these teachers often reference Christ and selected Scripture, it's a new image of Christianity they're peddling, one not bound to the archaic, restrictive, narrow beliefs and practices of your grandparents' faith. (We're more enlightened now.) The world has changed. Rachel Held Evans, for example, has unashamedly doubted "the Bible's exclusive authority, inerrancy, perspicuity, and internal consistency."[22] Even the government has woken up to the plight of the morally and sexually oppressed, passing legislation and declaring edicts to ensure that anyone standing in the way of "social progress" and "equality" will be squeezed out of the market-place, kicked to culture's curb, and silenced.

Naturally, as disciples of Jesus, we are convinced that *Scripture alone*, not attractive teachers in whatever form they come, is the final word on truth, history, and where it's headed. As such, those who follow Christ are the ones who will end up on the right(eous) side of history, right beside Him when He comes in glory.[23] In the meantime, the waters of apostasy continue to rise. And what's at stake is the very nature and definition of Christianity itself. But it's not simply the *institution* of Christianity that is at risk here. It's the *soul* of our faith.

What makes the Christian faith distinct from every other religion, belief system, and personal philosophy is the person of Jesus Christ. Detract from who He is in even the most minute way, and you have just veered onto the apostasy on-ramp. Because He alone accomplished salvation and rose from the dead, He definitively proved His deity. Therefore, every word He uttered, whether recorded in the Old Testament, spoken by Him while on earth, or inspired by His Spirit in the New Testament, becomes undeniable and unchangeable. And every prophetic word of His will be fulfilled, all the way down to the last and smallest letter. As Jesus Himself claimed, "Do not think that I came to abolish the Law or the Prophets; I did not come to abolish but to fulfill. For truly I say to you, until heaven and earth pass away, not the *smallest letter or stroke* shall pass from the Law until *all* is accomplished."[24] That's quite a declaration, rich with dramatic prophetic implications.

Still, today's apostates, and those who flirt with heresy, carry on with their smooth-talking doublespeak. They can talk for hours and say nothing yet leave you with the impression they know what they're talking about. Subtly, yet clearly, they subvert, sabotage, and deny core doctrines and beliefs of the Christian faith such as these:

- The deity of Jesus Christ
- His substitutionary atonement on the cross
- Jesus as the only way to salvation and heaven
- Salvation by grace through faith
- The inerrancy and infallibility of Scripture
- The triune nature of God—Father, Son, and Holy Spirit
- The existence of a literal hell and eternal, conscious torment
- The supernatural creation of the universe, earth, and man as described in Genesis 1–2
- The prophetic nature of Scripture
- The return of Jesus Christ to earth[25]

And they do it all in the name of God and, of course, "love."

Some of those who are currently departing from the faith are fueled by a reliance on "impressions" and internal voices giving direction and declaring truth about God. This is not the same as the Holy Spirit's inner witness and guidance every believer enjoys. Rather, these voices and impressions are definitively described as an authoritative "word from the Lord."

John MacArthur writes,

> Does the Spirit of God move our hearts and impress
> us with specific duties or callings? Certainly, but
> He works through the Word of God to do that.
> Such experiences are in no sense prophetic or
> authoritative. They are not *revelation*, but the effect
> of *illumination*, when the Holy Spirit applies the
> Word to our hearts and opens our spiritual eyes to
> its truth. We must guard carefully against allowing
> our experience and our own subjective thoughts
> and imaginations to eclipse the authority and the
> certainty of the more sure Word.[26]

So yes, God does guide us internally. However, we believe direct, divine, authoritative revelation ended with the conclusion of the canon of Scripture. The book of Revelation was God's final revelation.[27] Therefore, claims of "new truth" or revelations from God must come from another source, be it fallibly human or deceptively demonic.[28] Again, our thoughts must be grounded in Scripture and dependent upon the illuminating ministry and witness of the Holy Spirit.[29]

Unfortunately, in our "direct feed" culture, yesterday's truth is seen as outdated. Every morning we awaken to a fresh Twitter feed. Online news and social-media sites like Facebook constantly provide new content, updating themselves in a never-ending supply of pictures and posts. So why shouldn't God give us fresh, up-to-the-minute revelation as well? After all, our generation demands it, right?

Because of our culture's conforming and persuasive influence in our thinking, Scripture no longer is "enough." This is why, for many professing Christians, opening the Bible is like scrolling through outdated Instagram pictures. They may evoke a warm, sentimental feeling but still be (subconsciously) viewed as "old news." And yet what these people fail to realize is that the Word of God is "living and active and sharper than any two-edged sword, and piercing as far as the division of soul and spirit, of both joints and marrow, and able to judge the thoughts and intentions of the heart."[30]

The concept of living, perpetual truth from God's Word has become lost in an age of fresh, fluid social-media interaction. We open our phones, and virtually everything has changed since two minutes ago. But we open our Bible, and it reads the same as it did two days, two months, two years, or two centuries ago! It all boils down to how we understand the nature of God's Word and its life-changing power. Almost every professing Christian owns a Bible, but how many have been adequately equipped and inspired to dive into it? Or perhaps we have become products of a generation that is either too busy, too lazy, or too distracted to take the time and energy necessary to study it.

In reality, the Bible is *more* up-to-date and relevant than your Twitter feed—and many times over, since God's Word not only evaluates what is currently happening in the world but also tells us what is going to happen *before* it happens! That's relevance on a whole new, fresh level.

We must guard ourselves from drifting away from the "sola scriptura" (Scripture alone) championed by the Protestant reformers. Today's Christian motto is more like "*sometimes* Scriptura" (accompanied by wherever my emotions, pursuit of happiness, and self-fulfillment lead me). Without an intentional return to the primacy of God's Word on a large scale, the church will succumb to apostasy and be plunged into lethargy, apathy, impurity, and spiritual slumber.[31] We are quickly becoming a church culture of activity, presentation, self-help, and sermonettes. Our love affair with self must end and a rekindled love for Jesus be put in its place. *This* is the revival you can pray for!

Because we live in an age of instant media gratification and shallow interaction, we must retrain our minds to engage Scripture and understand its amazing daily relevance and fresh application to our lives.

A DIFFERENT KIND OF DRIFTING

For others, this departure from the faith is more difficult to spot. In fact, read the doctrinal statements of many church pastors and leaders today, and you'll have a hard time finding points of disagreement. They all seem biblical and legit.

But there is much more to orthodoxy and integrity than doctrinal statements.

Not long ago, I (Jeff) was standing in line to board a plane on my way to a speaking engagement. Just ahead of me in line was a middle-aged man accompanied by a much younger man, around college age. The older gentleman was dressed in black from head to toe—black leather shoes, black slacks, black knit sweater, and slick black hair. The younger man accompanying him carried a large backpack that appeared full. The older fellow carried only a cell phone. I couldn't help but overhear their conversation, which was heated. Well, only one of them was actually talking. The college boy just stood there. It soon became clear, due to the nature of the older man's rebuke, that the younger guy was his personal assistant and had committed a grievous mistake. As he repeatedly pointed his finger at the younger man, the boss's face grew more and more red.

I remember thinking, *Any second now he's going to punch that kid.*

Finally, we boarded the plane, and the (very public) verbal flogging ended. Making my way to my seat, I was disheartened to discover that I would be flying near the man in black. The college kid was seated in the row behind him and across from me.

No worries, I thought. *I'll be asleep in five minutes anyway.*

And that's when I heard a woman's voice call out to the man.

"Well, hello, Pastor! I didn't know you were on this flight. What a coincidence. I just have to tell you how much I *loved* your message last week . . ." These introductory remarks were followed by a long string of compliments, platitudes, and praises.

The man in black's face brightened, and he smiled, immediately transitioning to "minister mode." The tone of his voice became soft as he nodded his head, acknowledging the woman's adulation. Meanwhile, the college boy was on the phone, presumably talking to the church office. Overhearing his conversation, I was able to ascertain that the "unpardonable sin" this young man had committed was forgetting to arrange for the church van to pick them up on their arrival at the airport. Completing his call, the whipped and defeated young man slumped in his seat and stared out the window.

This pastor may subscribe to the same essential beliefs and doctrines as I do. And I'm quite sure he would claim to be a committed follower of Jesus. Sadly, though, his character that day didn't get the memo.

Now, I don't pretend to know this man's heart. And it's possible he could have simply been having a very bad day, or there might have been other extenuating circumstances. I could have observed him at the one time all year when he lost his temper in public. It's God's job to sort that out.

But what I can say with confidence is that there are people, according to Jesus, who don't just have "snapshot moments" where they drift off the narrow road. Instead, they've left the map altogether, as their entire lives betray what they say they believe. For them, it's not just an isolated scene out of the movie but rather the entire film that reveals their true character and where their allegiance lies.

Jesus, after explaining to His followers the narrow road concept and the "few who find it," stated,

> Not everyone who says to Me, "Lord, Lord," will enter the kingdom of heaven, but he who does the will of My Father who is in heaven will enter. Many will say to Me on that day, "Lord, Lord, did we not prophesy in Your name, and in Your name cast out demons, and in Your name perform many miracles?" And then I will declare to them, "I never knew you; depart from Me, you who practice lawlessness."[32]

When the lost are called to stand before Christ at the Great White Throne Judgment, the full extent of apostasy will be revealed.[33] And among those He will reject are individuals *within* the church who will profess to have been Christians. While on earth, they professed Christ, even claiming to have participated in supernatural acts and experiences—prophesying, casting out demons, and performing miracles. Impressive religious résumé material, to be sure. But to this particular group of people, Christ will utter the most terrifying words ever heard by human ears.

"I NEVER KNEW YOU; DEPART FROM ME"

Salvation is all about a *relationship* with Jesus Christ. By definition, a Christian is one who knows Christ and is known by Him.[34] In the Matthew 7 passage quoted above, Jesus is saying that because of their departure from genuine faith,[35] they give evidence of having never experienced genuine salvation. They never had an actual relationship with Him, even though they appeared to do great Christian things. A facade of faith existed but not the reality behind it. As a result, He will cast them out of His presence. Similar warnings are given to those who have been "enlightened" and who have "tasted" the Word of God but who have subsequently "fallen away."[36]

These are the "tares among the wheat."[37] Wolves among the sheep. Weeds in the garden. They may look like disciples and even believe as the rest do. They are almost indistinguishable from other Christians as they seamlessly blend into the body of Christ now. But they are separated from any association with Him at the judgment. These are the *Judases*. False converts. Pretenders. Fakes. Counterfeits.[38]

And the saddest thing of all is that they don't even realize it.

Chief among these are the false teachers who lead thousands of others astray. They posture and position themselves as teachers of the truth and sometimes even as prophets, but Jesus says they are nothing more than "blind guides."[39] So blind, in fact, that they can neither see the truth nor admit their own failure to abide by it. Far from holding anything back, Jesus also calls these spiritual gurus and guides "sons of hell," "fools," "hypocrites," "whitewashed tombs," "serpents," and "sons of vipers." He also told them they would not enter the Kingdom of Heaven.[40]

So Jesus, tell us what You *really* think!

In his prophetic epistle, Jude also warns us about these false teachers:

When these people eat with you in your fellowship
meals commemorating the Lord's love, they are like
dangerous reefs that can shipwreck you. They are like
shameless shepherds who care only for themselves.
They are like clouds blowing over the land without
giving any rain. They are like trees in autumn that
are doubly dead, for they bear no fruit and have
been pulled up by the roots. They are like wild waves
of the sea, churning up the foam of their shameful
deeds. They are like wandering stars, doomed forever
to blackest darkness.[41]

Harsh language. Stinging speech. But the truth can be like that sometimes. That's because much is at stake when guarding the purity of Jesus' precious bride.

Among the top priorities of today's apostate teachers is to gather large numbers of followers, creating national and international ministries. And this is by design. Some high-profile celebrity pastors even persuade their churches to purchase thousands of copies of their books, costing in the hundreds of thousands of dollars, in order to artificially inflate sales to give a false impression of the book's success. This is a marketing/sales technique used to "prime the pump" and boost *individual* sales to guarantee the book a spot on the *New York Times* Best Seller List. It's a "play" sometimes used today in the world of megachurch pastors. Though it's not illegal, it's nevertheless deceptive and evidences an absence of godly integrity.

One of the by-products of this Christian celebrity cult and culture is that it preys (and depends) upon there being an ample supply of untrained and ill-equipped churchgoers. In other words, unsuspecting, innocent sheep. And sadly, this supply never runs out. When those in leadership roles or those in influential writing, speaking, or pastoral positions drift into the error of apostasy, they drag masses of gullible followers out to sea with them. And because many sincere pastors fail to actually equip their own people in biblical discernment, this tragic phenomenon is only growing. False teachers are smooth talkers and expert performers. They are adept at presentation, persuasion, entertainment, and psychological manipulation . . . for "Kingdom purposes," they would say. Many know exactly what they're doing, having meticulously planned out and structured their messages to massage the minds and emotions of those in attendance. They are very skilled at what they do. Sadly, their delivery and "demonstration of power" is often mistaken for a "movement of the Spirit."

Like their secular celebrity counterparts, they love (and crave) the attention and praise of people, with the bottom line often being the accumulation of wealth—lots of it. For some of these fame-seeking teachers, ministry equals money.[42] Unfortunately, they are often the very personalities at ministry or denomination conferences who are paraded up front and put on display as "successful." They use descriptors like "mega," "multi," and "massive" to describe their ministries. Though church size is no indicator of the Spirit's work or blessing, it is often a primary qualification for fulfilling such speaking roles. Sadly, the church has bought into the "bigger is better" philosophy of the world. Though there is nothing intrinsically spiritual about a small church or inherently heretical about a big one, there is a value and *currency* being exchanged here. "Big" more and more often equals "success" and "God's favor." As a result, you won't likely see many small-church pastors, no matter how gifted or godly, speaking at these events.

Neglected and almost forgotten at such conferences are words like *faithful*, *sacrifice*, *suffering*, *disciple*, and *servant*. The one success these false teachers have achieved for certain is that they have augmented the Word of God to fit and facilitate a last-days generation—one that values above all the unholy trinity of Self, Size, and Silver.

But Jesus calls such people thieves, robbers, and hired hands. And they are assuredly *not* shepherds.[43]

THANK GOD FOR THE REAL DEAL

What a stark contrast these forgeries of faith are to authentic ministers. And thankfully, authentic ministers do exist. Look at 1 Thessalonians 2:1-9, and see how Paul's refreshing example compares to some of the self-obsessed Christian communicators today:

> You yourselves know, brethren, that our coming
> to you was not in vain, but after we had already

suffered and been mistreated in Philippi, as you
know, we had the boldness in our God to speak
to you the gospel of God amid much opposition.
For our exhortation does not come from error or
impurity or by way of deceit; but just as we have
been approved by God to be entrusted with the
gospel, so we speak, not as pleasing men, but God
who examines our hearts. For we never came with
flattering speech, as you know, nor with a pretext for
greed—God is witness—nor did we seek glory from
men, either from you or from others, even though
as apostles of Christ we might have asserted our
authority. But we proved to be gentle among you,
as a nursing mother tenderly cares for her own
children. Having so fond an affection for you, we
were well-pleased to impart to you not only the
gospel of God but also our own lives, because you
had become very dear to us.

For you recall, brethren, our labor and hardship,
how working night and day so as not to be a
burden to any of you, we proclaimed to you the
gospel of God.

To the Corinthians, Paul proclaimed, "You see, we are
not like the many hucksters who preach for personal profit.
We preach the word of God with sincerity and with Christ's
authority, knowing that God is watching us."[44]

Hucksters and peddlers, like the carnival barkers of old. Spiritual "snake oil salesmen."

Not Paul. His message and ministry were marked by humility, simplicity, and a true demonstration of the Spirit's power. And why? So that the Corinthians' faith would not rest on the wisdom, persuasion, and personality of a man but rather on the power of God.[45]

Paul was a man whose life was transformed by the risen Christ. And his faithful example is still being followed by godly people today. Those whom Jesus calls and equips to shepherd and speak, whether it be within the church or at large, are marked by a distinguishing characteristic—a burning passion to promote *Jesus'* name, not their own.[46] It is His fame they seek as they preach, teach, and serve. They subscribe to John the Baptist's motto: "He must increase, but I must decrease."[47]

They are men and women of the Word who possess a commitment to both doctrinal and personal integrity. They care nothing for people's praise but are content to please God alone with reverential honor. They don't "sweet talk" their audiences for contributions. They don't minister for awards, recognition, or human glory but for a future crown.[48] They are far more concerned with the health of the church than they are the size of it and more focused on faith than finances. And no matter the particulars of their church or ministry, they simply desire to be good *custodians* of it. Their joy is found in being faithful.

In heaven, those receiving the greatest rewards from

Christ just may be men and women you've never heard of. What do you think?

No matter what our areas of service in God's Kingdom, we must all see ourselves as stewards, loyal servants managing the influence, authority, and platform given us by God.[49] We must be mindful to never use that authority to dominate others or lead them astray.

That's because God's true leaders are gentle. Like nursing mothers, they treat people and their needs with tenderness. They understand the biblical balance of imparting both truth *and* life through real relationships. And if necessary, they are even willing to make costly personal sacrifices for the sake of the gospel and for those to whom they minister. Their motivation is a compelling call and a consuming love for their Lord Jesus Christ. And they are well aware that there is a "stricter judgment" for those who teach.[50]

This then is the antithesis of the self-serving doctrines and practices of today's apostasy.

I thank God for those who choose biblical integrity over popularity and expediency. They are authentic, dedicated disciples of Jesus, and the banner of faithfulness flies strong over them. Choose such people as your mentors, pastors, and teachers. These godly few. These servants of the Most High.

And strive to *be* one yourself.

CHAPTER 10

SURVIVING THE LAST DAYS OF APOSTASY

SEVERAL YEARS AGO, Tommy Nelson, pastor of Denton Bible Church, wrote an article in a publication from Dallas Theological Seminary titled "'Classic' Christianity." In the article he notes that "for several generations leading up to the 1960s, Coca-Cola was clearly the dominant soft drink in America." In a savvy marketing move, Pepsi decided to target the younger generation and let Coke continue to dominate the market for the older generations.

By the 1980s, Coke was losing market share to Pepsi, so in an effort to regain ground against Pepsi with the younger generation, Coca-Cola reformulated its flagship drink, branding it "New Coke." New Coke was sweeter and introduced as the "new taste of Coca-Cola." Coke's move was hailed as the biggest risk in consumer goods history. And if you're old enough to remember New Coke, you'll know that it was undoubtedly one of the greatest marketing missteps ever.

A fierce backlash from loyal Coke drinkers ensued. Angry calls and letters poured into Coke headquarters. The fans of Coke liked the old formula and didn't want it to change.

The day New Coke was announced, PepsiCo gave their employees the day off, saying, "By today's action, Coke has admitted that it's not the real thing." Pepsi was confident they were poised to dominate the market. Coke had compromised and changed.

Nelson describes what happened next: "But then Coke made what was called the greatest stroke of marketing genius in history. They apologized nationally, saying they realized that Coke was an American institution. They pulled New Coke off the shelves and brought back the original formula under the name of Classic Coke.

Nelson writes, "That name was not only a signal to the soft drink market that the familiar Coke had come back, *but it was also a recognition of the fact that when you have a classic, you don't change it just because of the pressure of a new generation.*"[1]

I (Mark) love that last sentence because that's the basic message of this book. Again and again, from different angles, we've highlighted the authority and sufficiency of the truth in God's Word and the centrality and exclusivity of the gospel of Jesus Christ. We have the classic. We have the real thing.

Any attempt to distort, dilute, or deny it will lead to the spiritual equivalent of Coke's marketing catastrophe.

Our calling is to stick to the classic.

HEY, JUDE

In the final New Testament book before the unfolding of the book of Revelation, Jude, the half brother of Jesus, calls all followers of Jesus to cling to "classic Christianity" and contend for it:

> Dear friends, I had been eagerly planning to write to you about the salvation we all share. But now I find that I must write about something else, urging you to defend the faith that God has entrusted once for all time to his holy people. I say this because some ungodly people have wormed their way into your churches, saying that God's marvelous grace allows us to live immoral lives. The condemnation of such people was recorded long ago, for they have denied our only Master and Lord, Jesus Christ.[2]

The book of Jude has been called the "Acts of the Apostates" by some. He soberly warns that apostates will mingle with God's people, pretending to be true believers. In light of this ever-present danger, followers of Jesus are to "defend" or "contend" for the faith. The word Jude uses for *defend* in the original language carries the idea of the strenuous, intense struggle expended in a wrestling match. Every believer in Christ is to contend for "the faith," that is, the orthodox body of truth and doctrine contained in God's Word.[3] Notice how the faith was delivered. It was entrusted and delivered to us by God with certainty and finality—"once for all time"—in His Word. No addition or alteration is ever needed. We have the classic.

Contending for the faith doesn't mean we have to be contentious or angry, but it does mean we must stand up for it. Yet far too many today are caving, not contending. The siren song of our culture is to water down the truth or simply omit the parts that may not go down smoothly.

I'm reminded of the young preacher who began his ministry at a new church. He preached the first Sunday on the dangers of drinking alcohol. After the service, one of the deacons approached him and said, "One-third of our people raise barley and distill alcohol, so I would be careful if I were you."

The next Sunday, the young pastor preached against smoking. The same deacon came up after the service and told him, "One-third of our members grow tobacco, so you'd better be careful."

The third Sunday, the sermon was on the perils of gambling. Again, after the service the same deacon pulled him aside. "One-third of our people raise thoroughbred horses, so you need to be more sensitive."

The following Sunday, the sermon title was "The Danger of Deep-Sea Diving in International Waters." He got the message loud and clear. But we must not cave to the pressures from our culture; we must contend for the faith.

Jude has often been described as the foyer or vestibule to the book of Revelation. Jude vividly describes the conditions that will prevail in the professing church in the final days before the events of the end times commence. His letter is another witness that the rise of apostasy is a sign of the times, portending the arrival of the end of days.

After his brief introduction in verses 1-3, verses 4-16 issue a strong denunciation of apostate false teachers who have wormed their way into the churches Jude addresses. To underscore those churches' danger, Jude gives three corporate examples of past apostasy (the wilderness generation, angels who sinned, and the cities of Sodom and Gomorrah) and three individual illustrations of apostasy from the Old Testament (Cain, Balaam, and Korah). Jude leaves no doubt about the disobedience and doom of all who turn from the truth and attempt to pull others into their wake.

HOW SHOULD WE THEN LIVE?

Beginning in verse 17, Jude shifts suddenly from the false teachers to the true followers. He sharply contrasts his readers with the apostates he's been describing and denouncing in verses 4-16. Jude 1:17 begins, "But you, beloved." The same words are found again in verse 20. He's telling us our duty in days of apostasy. As a loving pastor, Jude isn't just concerned with denouncing apostates. He wants to support and strengthen believers surrounded by apostasy. If we want to know how to survive in the last days of apostasy, Jude

1:17-25 gives us clear instruction. In these verses, Jude lays out four simple directives to equip his readers and us.

Remember

The first thing Jude tells us to do in days of apostasy is *remember*: "But you, beloved, ought to remember the words that were spoken beforehand by the apostles of our Lord Jesus Christ, that they were saying to you, 'In the last time there will be mockers, following after their own ungodly lusts.'"[4] Jude is telling us that apostasy shouldn't surprise us. Apostasy was predicted by all the apostles.[5] While departure from the truth should sadden us, it shouldn't surprise us. We need to remember the apostles told us it would come.

Remain

Along with remembering, believers must also *remain* or stand firm in our own spiritual growth: "But you, beloved, building yourselves up on your most holy faith, praying in the Holy Spirit, keep yourselves in the love of God, waiting anxiously for the mercy of our Lord Jesus Christ to eternal life."[6] These verses contain four things every believer must do to stand strong in the midst of the falling away.

First, we are to continually build ourselves up in the most holy faith. How do we do this? By faithful study of God's Word, which contains the truth of "the faith." The pure truth of God's Word builds us up spiritually and strengthens us to stand in difficult days.

Second, believers must pray in the Holy Spirit. Our prayer

life must be consistent and must be prompted, controlled, and guided by the Holy Spirit who indwells us.[7]

Third, we must keep ourselves in the love of God. This does not mean we must keep God loving us. God loves His children and will never stop. Nothing can separate us from His love for us.[8] However, when we sin, we can keep ourselves from experiencing and enjoying His love. The love of God is like sunshine that never ends, but our sin is like an umbrella we put up in our lives that keeps us from fully enjoying the love of God. We abide in God's love by obeying Him.[9]

Fourth, as we witness the widespread departure around us, we're to anxiously anticipate the coming of Jesus Christ. As someone said years ago, "The darker the outlook, the brighter the uplook!" God's people are not defeatists. We are the ultimate optimists. Jesus may be coming soon. All the signs we see around us are like runway lights signaling the approach of our Savior. Our task as we wait for the end times to arrive is to live for Christ in the meantime, committed to a life of studying, praying, obeying, and looking as we await our Lord's coming.

Reach Out

After we secure our own spiritual health and stability, Jude calls us to lovingly *reach out* to those around us who are the victims of the false teachers. Jude highlights three groups of people that need help.

The first group is the *doubters*. Verse 22 states, "Have mercy on some, who are doubting." In days of falling away and departure from the truth, we are surrounded by believers who are confused, wavering, and hesitating. False teachers prey upon the weak. I meet professing Christians regularly who struggle with all sorts of doubts about the truth of the Bible, the exclusivity of Jesus, the nature of God, and the meaning of life. For those drowning in doubt and confusion, we're to meet them with compassion and mercy.

Second, we need to reach out to the *deceived*. Verse 23 says, "Save others, snatching them out of the fire." The only other time Jude uses the word "fire" is in verse 7, which refers to the fire of judgment, so I believe the same meaning is intended here. These are people in great spiritual peril. When sound doctrine is under siege, as it is today, we need to be on the lookout for those who are deceived and to allow God to use us to share the gospel with them so they can be snatched out of the fire. Their false ideologies must be confronted and exposed by the power of God's truth.[10]

The final group who needs the touch of God's people is the *defiled*. Verse 23 tells us, "On some have mercy with fear, hating even the garment polluted by the flesh." These are people who have been overcome, contaminated, and polluted by the filth of this world. As moral standards, even within churches, continue to slide, moral apostasy will hold more and more people in its clutches. The sins of the culture inevitably become the sins of the church. For those overtaken by sin, we're to have mercy on them with compassion. But Jude adds this caveat: "hating even the garment polluted by the flesh." The "garment polluted by the flesh" literally refers to undergarments soiled by human excretions. This means we're to have an aversion or loathing for the sin in other people's lives just as we would hate to handle someone else's dirty underwear. We're to have a healthy fear of sin and maintain a wariness of getting too close to prevent our own defilement. Dealing with sin requires caution and a healthy fear.

Rest

The final condition for surviving the last days of apostasy is for us to *rest*. I love this. Jude ends this dark, stormy letter with a calming doxology of our safety and security in Christ: "Now to Him who is able to keep you from stumbling, and to make you stand in the presence of His glory blameless with great joy, to the only God our Savior, through Jesus Christ our Lord, be glory, majesty, dominion and authority, before all time and now and forever. Amen."[11] Like bookends, Jude begins and ends his letter highlighting our security in Christ.[12]

No true believer can apostatize from the faith. A believer may be confused, struggle with sin, and even believe some wrong things, but we can never lose our standing before God. He has the power to keep us from falling. He will see us through all the way to the end, when we stand in His glorious presence. But you are only secure if you have a personal relationship with God through faith in His Son, Jesus Christ.

KNOWN TO BE SAVED

In 1912, when the *Titanic* sank in the North Atlantic, 1,517 people met their demise in a watery grave. Once word of the tragedy got out, everyone wanted to know whether their loved ones had been saved. To aid those who had gathered to find news of their loved ones' fate, the White Star Line office in Liverpool, England, put up a big board divided in two with a heading on each side: "Known to Be Saved" and "Known to Be Lost." Hundreds watched with bated breath as each news report was recorded on the board.

The *Titanic*'s passengers had registered as first, second, or third class, but after the shipwreck, only two categories had any meaning: the living and the dead. The same will be true someday when the Lord comes. In the end, there will be only two classes: the saved and the lost—those who turned from self to Jesus Christ for salvation and those who did not. First John 5:12 draws the line of demarcation clearly: "He who has the Son has the life; he who does not have the Son of God does not have the life."

In spite of a rash of modern denials about the existence of hell, there are only two eternal destinations—heaven or hell. Jesus, the loving Savior who died for a world of sinners, unequivocally spoke of hell as the final destiny of those who reject Him.

Above all else, make sure you are among those "known to be saved." Make sure you have received Jesus as your Savior from sin. Make sure you know your final destination.

John 1:12 puts this as simply as possible. "As many as received Him, to them He gave the right to become children of God, even to those who believe in His name." Eternal life, forgiveness, and entrance into God's family come through simple faith and trust in Jesus Christ, the One who died in your place on the cross and rose again from the dead.[13]

You can trust Jesus now by calling upon Him to save you from your sins and by receiving the free gift of eternal life.

ORDERS REMAIN UNCHANGED

Of all the landmarks to see in our nation's capital, the Tomb of the Unknown Soldier in Arlington National Cemetery is one of the most profound. This is due in part to the constant, watchful guard that a platoon of thirty soldiers undertakes. Each day since 1937, every hour of the day, through all weather (including hurricanes) and every holiday, a single soldier has walked exactly 21 steps, then paused for 21 seconds before doing it again. The precision of the number 21 corresponds to the 21-gun-salute, the highest honor a soldier can receive. When the guard's watch is finished and a new guard comes on duty, the orders pass in three simple words: "Orders remain unchanged."

As the storm clouds gather and grow darker and the coming of Christ nears, these words—"orders remain unchanged"—should echo in our hearts and minds. We have our final marching orders from our Savior as we await His return:

Jesus came up and spoke to them, saying, "All authority has been given to Me in heaven and on earth. Go therefore and make disciples of all the nations, baptizing them in the name of the Father and the Son and the Holy Spirit, teaching them to observe all that I commanded you; and lo, I am with you always, even to the end of the age."[14]

Many things will change in our lives and in our ministries over the years. But one thing must never change—our commitment to the classic. We must never waver in our allegiance to Jesus and our dedication to spread His gospel and teach people all that He commanded. Our world doesn't need "New Coke." It needs the one thing that only God's Word can give it—the unchangeable, unchanging truth of God.

NOTES

INTRODUCTION

1. The exact etymology of the term *sabotage* is uncertain. This is one view.
2. See David Jeremiah, *God in You* (Sisters, OR: Multnomah, 1998), 73–74.
3. Genesis 3:1.
4. Jeremiah, *God in You*, 75.
5. Ibid.

CHAPTER 1: GOD AND GHOST SHIPS

1. "Shock Poll: Startling Numbers of Americans Believe World Now in the 'End Times,'" Religion News Service, September 11, 2013, http://pressreleases .religionnews.com/2013/09/11/shock-poll-startling-numbers-of-americans -believe-world-now-in-the-end-times.
2. Aamer Madhani, "Several Big U.S. Cities See Homicide Rates Surge," *USA Today*, July 10, 2015, http://www.usatoday.com/story/news/2015/07/09 /us-cities-homicide-surge-2015/29879091/.
3. "Number of Abortions—Abortion Counters," *US Abortion Clock.org*, accessed August 10, 2016, http://www.numberofabortions.com.
4. See Isaiah 5:20; Judges 21:25.
5. Bob Unruh, "Psychiatrists Seek to Destigmatize Adult-Child Sex," *WND*, August 22, 2011, http://www.wnd.com/2011/08/336869.
6. "Global Risks 2014 Insight Report," World Economic Forum, http://reports.weforum.org/global-risks-2014.
7. Kim Hjelmgaard, "Ten Greatest Threats Facing the World in 2014," *USA Today*, January 16, 2014, http://www.usatoday.com/story/news /world/2014/01/16/wef-biggest-risks-facing-world-2014/4505691.
8. See Revelation 13:16-17.

9. "2015 World Hunger and Poverty Facts and Statistics," *World Hunger Education Service*, http://www.worldhunger.org/articles/Learn/world%20hunger%20facts%202002.htm#Number_of_hungry_people_in_the_world.

10. "New ILO Global Estimate of Forced Labour: 20.9 Million Victims," *International Labour Organization*, June 1, 2012, http://www.ilo.org/global/topics/forced-labour/news/WCMS_182109/lang--en/index.htm.

11. Joshua Teitelbaum and Michael Segall, "The Iranian Leadership's Continuing Declarations of Intent to Destroy Israel, 2009-2012," *The Jerusalem Center for Public Affairs*, http://jcpa.org/wp-content/uploads/2012/05/IransIntent2012b.pdf.

12. This war, commonly called "The Battle of Gog and Magog," will involve a massive invasion of Islamic nations aligning themselves with Russia and its leader. Their objective will be to annihilate Israel. However, God will supernaturally intervene, rescuing his covenant people for his glory. See Ezekiel 38–39.

13. For a more detailed examination of this, see Mark Hitchcock, *Iran and Israel* (Eugene, OR: Harvest House, 2013).

14. Greg Botelho, "Police: FBI Probing Past of Suspect in Oklahoma Beheading," *CNN*, September 27, 2014, http://www.cnn.com/2014/09/26/us/oklahoma-beheading.

15. Catherine Herridge, "Army Warns US Military Personnel on ISIS Threat to Family Members," *Fox News*, October 2, 2014, http://www.foxnews.com/politics/2014/10/02/army-warns-us-military-personnel-on-isis-threat-to-family-members.

16. "Military Experts: With ISIS in El Paso, Ft. Bliss in Danger of Terrorist Attack," *Judicial Watch* (blog), September 4, 2014, http://www.judicialwatch.org/blog/2014/09/military-experts-isis-el-paso-ft-bliss-danger-terrorist-attack.

17. "Terrorist Training Camps in the US," *Military.com*, February 18, 2009, http://www.military.com/video/operations-and-strategy/domestic-terrorism/terrorist-training-camps-in-the-us/660940716001.

18. Douglas Ernst, "ISIL to U.S.: 'We will raise the flag of Allah in the White House,'" *Washington Times*, August 8, 2014, http://www.washingtontimes.com/news/2014/aug/8/isil-us-we-will-raise-flag-allah-white-house. In October of 2015, FBI Director James Comey stated that there were at least nine hundred active investigations into jihadist (ISIS-related) activity on American soil. The FBI is investigating ISIS-related activity in all fifty US states, meaning that ISIS has a network of supporters and sympathizers in every state in the union. See Kevin Johnson, "Anxiety Grows over ISIL Recruits in U.S.," *USA Today*,

November 14, 2015, http://www.usatoday.com/story/news/2015/11/14/isil-recruits-in-us-worry-officials/75774094.

19. 2 Corinthians 13:5. See also 1 Corinthians 10:12.

20. 2 Peter 1:10-11. All the important qualities Peter refers to in this opening chapter (verses 5-9) stem from a believer's authentic experience with the Word of God (verses 3-4).

21. See Acts 27:27-44; 2 Corinthians 11:25-26.

22. 1 Timothy 1:18-20, emphasis added.

23. See Hebrews 12:4-11.

24. See Matthew 7:21-27.

25. 1 John 2:4.

26. See Revelation 2:4.

27. See Ephesians 2:1-3.

28. Matthew 6:33. See also Psalm 37:4; Proverbs 3:5-6.

29. See 2 Corinthians 11:1-3; Ephesians 4:3.

30. 2 Timothy 3:16, emphasis added.

31. Matthew 16:18.

32. See Philippians 1:6.

33. See John 18:2.

34. John 17:15-16. See 2 Corinthians 4:4.

35. John 17:17.

36. See Galatians 1:6-9; 3:1-4; 5:1, 7-12.

CHAPTER 2: THE FIFTH COLUMN

1. George Sweeting, "Betrayal in the Church," *Moody* (April 1992): 74.

2. A.W. Tozer, *Man: The Dwelling Place of God* (Camp Hill, PA: WingSpread, 2008), 118.

3. Andy Woods, "The Last Days Apostasy of the Church (Part 1)," *Bible Prophecy Blog*, November 19, 2009, http://www.bibleprophecyblog.com/2009/11/last-days-apostasy-of-church-part-1.html.

4. Examples of personal apostasy are found in the serious warnings of Hebrews 6:4-8 and 10:26-31.

5. Titus 1:16.

6. See Revelation 13:1-18; 17:11-15.

7. See Genesis 11:1-9; Revelation 13:4.

8. See Daniel 9:27; Ezekiel 38:8, 11.

9. See 1 Thessalonians 5:1-3; Revelation 6:1-4.

10. Woods, "Last Days."

11. See Acts 18:1-11.

12. 2 Thessalonians 2:1-2, ESV.

13. See 1 Thessalonians 1:9-10; 4:17; 5:1-9.

14. That the Thessalonians were so upset by the teaching that they were in the Day of the Lord indicates this was not something they were expecting. This lends support to the pre-Tribulation timing of the Rapture. If the Thessalonians believed they would have to endure the Tribulation before Christ's coming, then why would they have been so upset to receive a letter telling them the Day of the Lord had come? They would have been excited, not shaken and afraid. This would mean that what Paul had taught them was being fulfilled. They would have faced the Tribulation with hope and endurance, knowing that the coming of the Lord was less than seven years away. But their response was the exact opposite. They were "shaken from their composure" and "disturbed." The spurious letter they had received contradicted what Paul had taught them in 1 Thessalonians 4–5. It either meant that Paul had lied to them before about the pre-Trib Rapture, they had totally misunderstood what he said, or the Rapture had already come and they had been left behind. Any of these scenarios was devastating. The only logical conclusion from 2 Thessalonians 2:1-2 is that from Paul's previous teaching in 1 Thessalonians, the Thessalonians must have believed that the Rapture would occur before the beginning of the Tribulation. Paul went on in 2 Thessalonians 2:3-11 to show the believers that the teaching that they were already in the Day of the Lord was false doctrine and that their fears of being in this awful period were groundless. For a thorough discussion of the timing of the Rapture, see Mark Hitchcock, *The End* (Carol Stream, IL: Tyndale, 2012).

15. Charles R. Swindoll, *Steadfast Christianity: A Study of Second Thessalonians*, Bible Study Guide (Anaheim, CA: Insight for Living, 1986), 23.

16. 2 Thessalonians 2:3, ESV.

17. Since the word *apostasia* means "departure," some have understood the term "the apostasy" to be the physical departure of the church itself—that is, the Rapture, since the Rapture will be a physical departure of believers from the earth. If this view were correct, it would definitely place the Rapture before the Tribulation, which would be a slam dunk for the pre-Tribulation Rapture position. While this is attractive to pretribulationists, there are six main reasons to reject a physical departure as the meaning of *apostasia* in this context: (1) In classical Greek, *hē apostasia* ("the apostasy") was used to denote a political or military rebellion. (2) In the Septuagint (the Greek translation of the Old Testament), this term was used of rebellion against God (see Joshua 22:22; Jeremiah 2:19). (3) In 2 Maccabees 2:15 (a noncanonical book written in the time between the Old and New Testaments), it is used of apostasy to paganism. (4) In Acts 21:21, the only

other use of the noun in the New Testament, it refers to apostasy or spiritual departure from Moses. (5) The Rapture is not an act of departure by the saints; the saints are passive not active participants. (6) In 2 Thessalonians 2:1, Paul refers to the Rapture as "our gathering together to Him." It seems strange to use this unlikely term ("the apostasy") for the same thing in the immediate context. (These six points are from D. Edmond Hiebert, *1 & 2 Thessalonians* (Chicago: Moody Press, 1971), 331. For these reasons, most expositors have understood "the rebellion" (apostasy) not as the physical departure of the church at the Rapture but rather as doctrinal, theological, and moral departure from the truth.

18. F. F. Bruce, *1 & 2 Thessalonians*, Word Biblical Commentary, gen. ed. David A. Hubbard and Glenn W. Barker, vol. 45 (Waco, TX: Word Books, 1982), 166. See also Leon Morris, *1 and 2 Thessalonians*, Tyndale New Testament Commentaries, rev. ed. (Grand Rapids, MI: Eerdmans, 1989), 127.

19. John Calvin, *1 & 2 Thessalonians,* Crossway Classic Comentaries, ed. Alister McGrath and J. I. Packer (Wheaton, IL: Crossway, 1999), 86–87.

20. G. K. Beale, *1-2 Thessalonians*, IVP New Testament Commentary Series, ed. Grant R. Osborne (Downers Grove, IL: InterVarsity Press, 2003), 204. Beale provides several convincing points to support his view.

21. 2 Thessalonians 2:4, ESV.

22. John R. W. Stott, *The Message of 1 & 2 Thessalonians* (Downers Grove, IL: InterVarsity Press, 1991), 158.

23. Charles Ryrie, *First and Second Thessalonians* (Chicago: Moody, 1959), 103–104.

24. Homer A. Kent, Jr., *The Pastoral Epistles*, rev. ed. (Chicago: Moody, 1986), 143.

25. Mal Couch, gen. ed., *A Biblical Theology of the Church* (Grand Rapids, MI: Kregel, 1999), 110.

26. John Phillips, *Exploring the Future: A Comprehensive Guide to Bible Prophecy* (Grand Rapids, MI: Kregel, 2003), 225, 269.

27. John F. Walvoord, *The Church in Prophecy* (Grand Rapids, MI: Zondervan, 1964), 66.

28. Ibid., 50.

29. J. Dwight Pentecost, *Will Man Survive?* (Grand Rapids, MI: Zondervan, 1980), 58.

30. John Harold Ockenga, quoted in "Apostasy," Paul Lee Tan Prophetic Ministries, http://www.tanbible.com/tol_ill/apostasy.htm.

31. Donald Grey Barnhouse, *Thessalonians: An Expository Commentary* (Grand Rapids, MI: Zondervan, 1977), 98.

32. John Horsch, *Modern Religious Liberalism* (Scottdale, PA: Fundamental Truth Depot, 1921), 322.

CHAPTER 3: FAITH OF OUR FATHERS

1. Genesis 3:5.
2. 2 Timothy 3:16-17, NLT.
3. See John 15:18-27.
4. In an interview on Oprah Winfrey's *Super Soul Sunday*, Bell said, "We're moments away. I think the culture is already there. And the church will continue to be even more irrelevant when it quotes letters from 2,000 years ago as their best defense." See "Rob Bell Suggests Bible Not Relevant to Today's Culture," *CBN News*, February 19, 2015, http://www1.cbn.com /cbnnews/us/2015/February/Rob-Bell-Suggests-Bible-Not-Relevant-to -Todays-Culture.
5. Jim Hinch, "Evangelicals Are Losing the Battle for the Bible. And They're Just Fine with That," *Los Angeles Review of Books*, February 15, 2016, http://lareviewofbooks.org/article/evangelicals-are-losing-the-battle-for -the-bible-and-theyre-just-fine-with-that.
6. Hebrews 5:14.
7. See 2 Peter 3:18.
8. See Titus 1:10–2:1.
9. See 1 Timothy 4:6.
10. See 2 Timothy 4:2-3.
11. See Titus 1:9; 1 Timothy 6:3-5.
12. John 4:22-24, NLT.
13. See Genesis 1:26. Being created in God's image involves possessing intellect (being able to think and reason), emotion (the capacity for feeling), and will (the ability to choose). It also means we are *spiritual* beings. Though we spiritually died in Adam's fall, we are made alive once again through Christ at salvation (see Ephesians 2:1, 5; Colossians 2:11-13; Titus 3:5).
14. See Romans 1:18-20; 2:14-15 concerning general revelation. See also Colossians 1:15-19; Hebrews 1:1-4 regarding special revelation through Jesus Christ.
15. John 4:23.
16. See Exodus 20:1-8. See also Exodus 32:1-6, where Israel portrayed its God as a golden calf. This false image of God not only insulted His glory but also led to all sorts of sin and debauchery.
17. 2 Corinthians 10:3-5.
18. See Matthew 4:1-11.
19. See 1 Corinthians 8:1.

20. Romans 1:21-22, emphasis added.
21. Romans 11:36.
22. Philippians 1:9-11, NIV, emphasis added.
23. Colossians 1:9-10, emphasis added.
24. John 17:3.
25. The word most often used to describe this knowledge is *ginóskó*, whose primary meaning is to know through personal experience. This experience begins with the mind and is translated to practical living.
26. See 1 Corinthians 13:12; 1 John 3:2-3.
27. See Ephesians 4:11-16.
28. Jude 1:3, emphasis added.
29. 1 Timothy 6:20; 2 Timothy 1:13, NLT.
30. 2 Timothy 1:14, NLT, emphasis added.
31. Jude 1:4.
32. "Theology" refers to the study of God. Specifically, the study of salvation is referred to as "soteriology," and the study of Christ, "Christology." These are terms used to help systematize and categorize Christian doctrine and teaching. Generally speaking, most systematic theologies break down as follows: prolegomena (introduction to general theology, how God reveals himself, etc.), bibliology (the study of the Bible), theology proper (the study of the doctrine of God), Christology (the study of Jesus Christ), pneumatology (the study of the Holy Spirit), anthropology (the study of humankind), soteriology (the study of salvation), ecclesiology (the study of the church), angelology (the study of angels and demons), and eschatology (the study of the end times).
33. See Proverbs 1:7.
34. See John 17:3, 17; Romans 3:4; Titus 1:2.
35. See John 14:26; 16:13-16.
36. See Ephesians 6:11, 14.
37. See 1 Peter 3:15.
38. Matthew 7:15-16, NLT.
39. See John 1:17-18; 14:6.
40. Here is an excellent list of Scriptures dealing with false teachers and our response to them: https://www.openbible.info/topics/exposing_false_teachers.
41. See Acts 17:11.
42. See Matthew 7:24-27.

CHAPTER 4: CULTURE OF COMPROMISE

1. Paul W. Powell, *Thee Old Time Religion* (Waco, TX: Paul W. Powell, 2001), 9.
2. Francis A. Shaeffer, *The Great Evangelical Disaster* (Wheaton, IL: Crossway, 1984), 64.

3. "Americans: My Faith Isn't the Only Way to Heaven," Associated Press, June 24, 2008, http://www.foxnews.com/story/2008/06/24/americans-my -faith-isnt-only-way-to-heaven.html.

4. See Romans 12:2.

5. A. W. Tozer, *Man: The Dwelling Place of God*, reprint (Camp Hill, PA: WingSpread, 2008), 188.

6. See Daniel 1:3-20.

7. See 2 Timothy 4:10.

8. See Hebrews 2:1-4.

9. See Hebrews 3:12.

10. See John 6:60, 66.

11. John Shore, "The Inevitability of the Rise of Progressive Christianity," *Patheos*, September 19, 2011, http://www.patheos.com/blogs/johnshore/2011/09 /the-inevitability-of-the-rise-of-liberal-christianity.

12. 2 Timothy 4:1-4.

13. Tim LaHaye and Jerry B. Jenkins, *Are We Living in the End Times?* (Carol Stream, IL: Tyndale, 1999), 71.

14. Rachel Held Evans, *A Year of Biblical Womanhood* (Nashville: Thomas Nelson, 2012), 54.

15. J. Carl Laney, *John* (Chicago: Moody, 1992), 156–157.

16. Trillia Newbell, "Biblical Womanhood and the Problem of the Old Testament," *Desiring God*, October 15, 2012, http://www.desiringgod.org /articles/biblical-womanhood-and-the-problem-of-the-old-testament.

17. See John 8:11.

18. John 7:7, NLT.

19. John 15:18-23, NLT.

20. Glennon Doyle Melton, "Are You Waiting for Heaven or Working for It?" *Momastery* (blog), March 29, 2016, http://momastery.com/blog/2016/03/29 /waiting-or-working.

21. See Matthew 7:13-14; John 3:36; 8:24.

CHAPTER 5: WHEN TOLERANCE IS INTOLERABLE

1. Jeremiah 17:9, NLT.

2. C. S. Lewis, *The Case for Christianity* (Nashville: Broadman and Holman, 2000), 32.

3. 1 John 3:16, NLT.

4. John 3:16, NLT.

5. Romans 5:8, NLT.

6. See 1 John 4:7-8.

7. See 1 John 4:19.

8. See Ephesians 5:25, 28-29.

9. 2 Peter 3:18.

10. "For the First Time, Starbucks Raises the Pride Flag atop Its Headquarters," *Starbucks Newsroom*, June 23, 2014, https://news.starbucks.com/news /for-the-first-time-starbucks-raises-the-pride-flag-atop-its-headquarters.

11. See John 1:9; 3:19-20; 8:12.

12. Isaiah 5:20.

13. Romans 1:24-28.

14. Romans 1:29-32, NLT.

15. See John 15:18-25.

16. John 6:37, NLT. See Mark 2:13-17; Luke 7:36-50; 19:1-10.

17. See Genesis 9:9-17.

18. See Genesis 6:1-13; Romans 1; 3:1-12, 23. For a more detailed explanation of the Flood judgment, Noah's generation, and their relationship to end-times prophecy, see Jeff Kinley, *As It Was in the Days of Noah: Warnings from Bible Prophecy about the Coming Global Storm* (Eugene, OR: Harvest House, 2014).

19. *The Safe Space Network*, http://safespacenetwork.tumblr.com/Safespace.

20. See Ephesians 4:32; Philippians 4:5.

21. Matthew 23:23, ESV. See also Matthew 9:13.

22. See 2 Corinthians 10:5.

23. See Romans 14.

24. Revelation 2:2, NLT. See Revelation 2:20.

25. Revelation 2:24.

26. See Romans 6:1-2, 15; Galatians 2:17-21; 5:13; 1 Peter 2:16.

27. Matthew 15:9.

28. Mark 7:6, NIV.

29. Matthew 23:27-28. See also Isaiah 29:13; Matthew 6:1-2; 23:24; Luke 16:15; Galatians 4:10-11; 5:2-4.

30. John 14:15.

31. See 2 Timothy 4:3-5; 2 Corinthians 4:4; Ephesians 2:2; 6:11; John 8:44.

32. Habakkuk 1:13, NIV.

33. God has a plan and a purpose for everything, even the existence of evil and evil men (see Romans 9:15-22; Proverbs 16:4; Deuteronomy 29:29). It is impossible to know all His reasons for allowing evil to exist, but we do know that He can turn sinful actions into good things for us and glory for Him (see Genesis 50:20; Acts 2:23; 4:27-28; Romans 8:28).

34. 2 Peter 3:9, NIV.

35. See Acts 14:15-17; Romans 3:24-25.

36. See Acts 17:24-25; 2 Corinthians 6:1-2.

37. Ephesians 5:16.

38. See 2 Timothy 2:2.

39. Greek *koinonia*—meaning a partnership or sharing together, a joint participation.

40. See Ephesians 2:20. 1 Peter 2:5; Hebrews 10:23-25.

CHAPTER 6: MORAL FREEFALL

1. This is adapted from John MacArthur's "The Conscience, Revisited," Grace to You, http://www.gty.org/resources/Articles/A273/The-Conscience -Revisited.

2. This joke is adapted from "100 Mile an Hour Goat," November 9, 2009, http://www.ebaumsworld.com/jokes/read/80809499.

3. A. W. Tozer, *Man: The Dwelling Place of God* (Camp Hill, PA: WingSpread, 2008), 181.

4. Read 2 Peter 2 and the Epistle of Jude, and you will see this pattern vividly illustrated.

5. 2 Timothy 3:1-5.

6. See Acts 2:17; Hebrews 1:1-2; 1 Peter 1:20; 1 John 2:18 ("the last hour").

7. Homer A. Kent Jr., *The Pastoral Epistles*, rev. ed. (Winona Lake, IN: BMH Books, 1986), 272.

8. John F. MacArthur, *1 & 2 Timothy*, in The MacArthur New Testament Commentary (Chicago: Moody, 1995), 107.

9. Ray C. Stedman, *The Fight of Faith: Studies in the Pastoral Letters of Paul, I and II Timothy and Titus* (Grand Rapids, MI: Discovery House, 2009), 238.

10. Don Carson, *From the Resurrection to His Return: Living Faithfully in the Last Days* (Tain, Scotland: Christian Focus, 2010), 18.

11. K. Edward Copeland, "Shadowlands: Pitfalls and Parodies of Gospel-Centered Ministry," in *Entrusted with the Gospel: Pastoral Expositions of 2 Timothy*, ed. D. A. Carson (Wheaton, IL: Crossway, 2010), 93–94.

12. This illustration is borrowed from Doug McIntosh, *Life's Greatest Journey: How to Be Heavenly Minded AND of Earthly Good* (Chicago: Moody Press, 2000), 13–14.

13. Philip DeCourcy, "You Don't Get to Write the Rules," *Know the Truth*, January 23, 2015, http://www.ktt.org/pages/page.asp?page_id=153644 &articleId=47346.

14. Ibid.

15. See 1 Thessalonians 1:9-10.

16. See 2 Thessalonians 2:2-3.

17. 2 Timothy 3:14-17, ESV.

18. See 2 Timothy 2:1; 3:10, 14; 4:5.

19. Every main passage in the New Testament on apostasy and false teaching is followed closely with a statement about God's Word. Here are a few examples: 1 Timothy 4:13-16; 2 Timothy 3:16-17; 2 Peter 1:21 (here the statement about Scripture precedes the warning about false teachers); 2 Peter 3:1-2; Jude 1:17.

20. Philip Graham Ryken, *He Speaks to Me Everywhere: Meditations on Christianity and Culture* (Phillipsburg, NJ: P & R Publishing, 2004), 17-18.

CHAPTER 7: THE WATERSHED MOMENT FOR THE CHURCH

1. Obergefell v. Hodges, 576 S. Ct. at 22 (2015).

2. The Associated Press, "Presbyterian Church Leaders Declare Gay Marriage Is Christian," *NBC News*, June 20, 2014, http://www.nbcnews.com /news/us-news/presbyterian-church-leaders-declare-gay-marriage-christian -n136256.

3. "Tony Campolo's Gay Marriage Support Highlights Divide," *CBN News*, June 12, 2015, http://www1.cbn.com/cbnnews/us/2015/June/Campolos -Gay-Marriage-Support-Highlights-Divide.

4. "Rob Bell Suggests Bible Not Relevant to Today's Culture," *CBN News*, February 19, 2015, http://www1.cbn.com/cbnnews/us/2015/February /Rob-Bell-Suggests-Bible-Not-Relevant-to-Todays-Culture.

5. Rachel Held Evans, "For the Sake of the Gospel, Drop the Persecution Complex," *Rachel Held Evans* (blog), July 15, 2015, http://rachelheldevans .com/blog/persecution-complex.

6. In one recent example, an influential blogger among evangelicals posted this message on Facebook: "After our beautiful, beautiful event today, a woman walked up to me and said: 'I have been waiting my entire life for someone in church to say the words you said today.' . . . I said . . . that it is high time Christians opened wide their arms, wide their churches, wide their tables, wide their homes to the LGBT community. So great has our condemnation and exclusion been, that gay Christian teens are SEVEN TIMES more likely to commit suicide. Nope. No. No ma'am. Not on my watch. No more. This is so far outside the gospel of Jesus that I don't even recognize its reflection. I can't. I won't. I refuse. So whatever the cost and loss, this is where I am: gay teens? Gay adults? Mamas and daddies of precious gaybees? Friends and beloved neighbors of very dear LGBT folks? Here are my arms open wide. . . . You matter so desperately and your life is worthy and beautiful. There is nothing 'wrong with you,' or in any case, nothing more right or wrong than any of us, which is to say

we are all hopelessly screwed up but Jesus still loves us beyond all reason and lives to make us all new, restored, whole." Posted April 23, 2016, https://www.facebook.com/permalink.php?story_fbid=946752262090436&id=203920953040241.

7. Christian Smith, *Soul Searching: The Religious and Spiritual Lives of American Teenagers* (New York: Oxford University Press, 2009), 171.
8. Ibid.
9. See 1 Peter 4:12-19.
10. See Romans 1:26-27.
11. See James 2:10-11.
12. See Genesis 19 (Sodom is catastrophically wiped out for its sin); Leviticus 18:22 (it's called an "abomination"); Leviticus 20:13 (it's punishable by death).
13. "Campolo's Gay Marriage Support," *CBN News*.
14. Glenn R. Kreider and Thomas M. Mitchell, "Kindness and Repentance: Romans 2:4 and Ministry to People with Same-Sex Attractions," *Bibliotheca Sacra* 173 (January–March 2016): 60.
15. See John Stott, *Same-Sex Partnerships? A Christian Perspective* (Grand Rapids, MI: Revell, 1998), 18.
16. Ibid., 22.
17. See Jude 1:6-7.
18. Kevin DeYoung, *What Does the Bible Really Teach about Homosexuality?* (Wheaton, IL: Crossway, 2015), 55.
19. Ibid., 63–65.
20. Ibid., 77.
21. Thomas E. Schmidt, *Straight & Narrow? Compassion & Clarity in the Homosexuality Debate* (Downers Grove, IL: InterVarsity Press, 1995), 64.
22. Peter Coleman, *Christian Attitudes to Homosexuality* (London: SPCK, 1980), 101.
23. Rod Dreher, "What If Rachel Held Evans Is Wrong?" *Real Clear Religion*, May 15, 2012, http://www.realclearreligion.org/articles/2012/05/15/what_if_rachel_held_evans_is_wrong_106490.html.
24. John Stott, *Same-Sex Partnerships?*, 54.
25. Ibid., 54–55.
26. See John 14:15; Romans 13:8.
27. Stott, *Same-Sex Partnerships?*, 57.
28. Stott, *Same-Sex Partnerships?*, 58.
29. See Leviticus 18:22; 20:13.
30. See Matthew 10:14-15; 11:23-24; Luke 10:10-12; 17:26-30.
31. Romans 1:32.

32. Thomas R. Schreiner, *Romans*, Baker Exegetical Commentary on the New Testament, ed. Moses Silva (Grand Rapids, MI: Baker Books, 1998), 99–100.

33. C. E. B. Cranfield, *The Epistle to the Romans*, The International Critical Commentary, gen. ed. J. A. Emerton and C. E. B. Cranfield, vol. 1 (Edinburgh: T&T Clark, 2006), 135.

34. Robert H. Mounce, *Romans*, The New American Commentary, gen. ed. E. Ray Clendenen, vol. 27 (Nashville: Broadman & Holman, 1995), 86.

35. Russell Goldman, "Here's a List of 58 Gender Options for Facebook Users," *ABC News*, February 13, 2014, http://abcnews.go.com/blogs /headlines/2014/02/heres-a-list-of-58-gender-options-for-facebook-users.

36. Luke 17:28-30.

37. Chelsen Vicari, "Jen Hatmaker, Blurry Lines, and Transformative Truth," *Faith & Chelsen* (blog), Patheos, April 26, 2016, http://www.patheos.com /blogs/faithchelsen/2016/04/jen-hatmaker-blurry-lines-and-transformative -truth. For an excellent presentation of our response to those with same-sex attraction, see Glenn R. Kreider and Thomas M. Mitchell, "Kindness and Repentance: Romans 2:4 and Ministry to People with Same-Sex Attractions," *Bibliotheca Sacra* 173 (January–March 2016): 57–79.

CHAPTER 8: WILL THE REAL JESUS STAND UP?

1. This version of "One Solitary Life" is adapted from James Allan Francis, "Arise Sir Knight!" in *The Real Jesus and Other Sermons* (Philadelphia: The Judson Press, 1926), 123–124.

2. Kenneth Humphreys, *Jesus Never Existed: An Introduction to the Ultimate Heresy* (Charleston, WV: Nine-Banded Books, 2014). This is, of course, a minority view, as very few credible secular historians actually doubt or deny the historicity of Jesus.

3. Warren Cole Smith, "A conversation with Bart Ehrman," *World*, January 9, 2015, https://world.wng.org/2015/01/a_conversation_with_bart_ehrman.

4. "What Do Americans Believe about Jesus?" Barna Group, April 1, 2015, https://www.barna.org/barna-update/culture/714-what-do-americans -believe-about-jesus-5-popular-beliefs#.VyJyHmPwB20.

5. See Revelation 1:4-18.

6. John 2:23-25. Their belief in Jesus could have been merely intellectual and not a volitional trust in Him. As a result, though they "believed" in Him, Jesus did not "believe" (same Greek word) in *them*.

7. See Isaiah 55:8-9; Romans 3:10-12; Ephesians 2:1-3. See also Romans 1:21; 1 Corinthians 2:14.

8. See John 14:16-17, 26; 16:13-14. See also Ephesians 1:17-18; 1 Corinthians 2:10-16.

9. Nicola Menzie, "5 False 'Messiahs' and Why Their Claims to Be Christ Contradict the Bible," *Church & Ministry*, The Christian Post, June 6, 2013, http://www.christianpost.com/news/5-false-messiahs-and-why-their-claims-to-be-christ-contradict-the-bible-97059.

10. Brian D. McLaren, *A New Kind of Christianity: Ten Questions That Are Transforming the Faith* (San Francisco: HarperOne, 2011), 139, emphasis added.

11. John 1:14. See also Romans 8:3; Philippians 2:7.

12. Hebrews 2:14, 17-18.

13. Hebrews 4:15.

14. See Romans 8:3; Hebrews 2:17; 4:14-16.

15. See John 1:14, 18; 2 Corinthians 5:21; Titus 2:14; Hebrews 7:25-27; 9:15.

16. Matthew 16:13-16, emphasis added.

17. Hebrews 13:8.

18. See Psalm 139:13-16.

19. Through "general revelation" (creation and conscience), we can understand that God is a divine being who is eternal, powerful, moral, and creative. But the specifics regarding the incarnate Christ we can know authoritatively only through Scripture.

20. Matthew 11:28 and Matthew 8:12.

21. For more on this topic, see Mark Hitchcock, *Visits to Heaven and Back: Are They Real?* (Carol Stream, IL: Tyndale, 2015).

22. See Revelation 12:9; 20:10.

23. Ephesians 4:14, NLT.

CHAPTER 9: ACTS OF THE APOSTATES

1. John 10:7, 11.

2. John 10:14, 27.

3. John 10:3, emphasis added.

4. See John 10:11.

5. Hebrews 13:20. See also 1 Peter 2:25.

6. Though the English word *pastor* (in its plural form) is translated as such only once in the New Testament (see Ephesians 4:11), the Greek word (*poimen*) is otherwise rendered "shepherd" seventeen times. In verb form, it is used three times to refer to leadership and overseeing God's people (see John 21:16; Acts 20:28; 1 Peter 5:2).

7. 1 Timothy 3:15, NIV. See 1 Timothy 5:17.

8. See 2 Thessalonians 2:6-7.

9. 1 Timothy 4:6.

10. 1 Timothy 4:13.

NOTES

11. 1 Timothy 4:15.
12. 1 Timothy 4:16.
13. 2 Timothy 4:1-5, NLT.
14. 1 Timothy 4:1, emphasis added.
15. See Hebrews 1:1-2; 9:26; 1 Peter 1:20; 1 John 2:18.
16. See Matthew 24:37; 2 Thessalonians 2:3-12; Hebrews 3:12; 5:11–6:8; 10:25; 2 Peter 3:3; Jude 1:18.
17. Revelation 12:9.
18. John 8:44; 2 Corinthians 4:4; Luke 11:15; Ephesians 6:12.
19. 2 Corinthians 11:13-15.
20. Glennon Doyle Melton, "Are You Waiting for Heaven or Working for It?" *Momastery* (blog), March 29, 2016, http://momastery.com/blog/2016/03/29/waiting-or-working.
21. This is precisely the kind of worldliness Paul warns the Roman believers about in Romans 12:1-2. It's an external pressure that forces us into a certain way of thinking and acting. It involves both values and behavior. And in a religious context, it often means "rethinking" the long-held historical beliefs of Christianity.
22. Rachel Held Evans, "Loving the Bible for What It Is, Not What I Want It to Be," *Rachel Held Evans* (blog), January 2, 2012, http://rachelheldevans.com/blog/bible-series.
23. See Revelation 19:11-16.
24. Matthew 5:17-18, emphasis added.
25. There are other dangerous doctrinal aberrations that do not directly call into question Christ's identity or the foundations of Christianity but that nevertheless deviate and depart from orthodox Christian belief. These "second tier" aberrations include beliefs and practices such as the prosperity gospel, the social gospel, the "second blessing," the word of faith movement, "name it and claim it," faith healers, the laughing movement, and the veneration of Mary and "saints."
26. John MacArthur, "False Prophets and Lying Wonders," *Grace to You*, accessed August 29, 2016, https://www.gty.org/resources/print/blog/B100111.
27. See Hebrews 1:1-2; Jude 1:3; Revelation 22:18-19.
28. There is no shortage today of these types of claims—from supposed visits to heaven to sensationalized revelations regarding prophecy and the end times. Some of these "words from God" are relatively trivial in nature, while others border on the bizarre.
29. See John 14:16-17, 26; 15:26; 16:13-14; Romans 8:9, 16.
30. Hebrews 4:12.
31. See Revelation 3:1-2.

32. Matthew 7:21-23.
33. See Revelation 20:11-15.
34. See John 10:14; 17:3; Philippians 3:8; 1 John 2:3; 5:20.
35. The word for "depart from" that Jesus uses in Matthew 7:23 is distinct from yet similar to the Greek word for *apostasy*. ἀποχωρέω comes from two words, *apo* ("from" or "away from") and *choreo* (to leave or go away, depart).
36. See Hebrews 6:4-6.
37. See Matthew 13:24-30.
38. See 1 John 2:19; Jude 1:20-24.
39. See Matthew 23:16, 17, 19, 24, 26.
40. See Matthew 23:13-36; Luke 11:52.
41. Jude 1:12-13, NLT.
42. See 1 Timothy 6:10.
43. See John 10:1-16.
44. 2 Corinthians 2:17, NLT.
45. See 1 Corinthians 2:1-5.
46. See Psalm 115:1; 2 John 1:7.
47. John 3:30.
48. See 1 Peter 5:2-4.
49. See 1 Corinthians 4:1-5.
50. James 3:1.

CHAPTER 10: SURVIVING THE LAST DAYS OF APOSTASY
1. Tommy Nelson, "'Classic' Christianity: Teaching and Living the Unchanging Truth of God's Word," *Veritas* (January 2008), http://www.dts.edu /download/publications/veritas/veritas-2008-january.pdf, emphasis added.
2. Jude 1:3-4, NLT.
3. See 1 Timothy 1:9; 4:1; 5:8; 6:10, 21; 2 Timothy 4:7.
4. Jude 1:17-18.
5. See 1 Timothy 4:1; 2 Timothy 3:1-13; 4:3; 1 John 2:18-19; 4:1-3; 2 Peter 2:1-2; 3:3-4.
6. Jude 1:20-21.
7. See also Ephesians 6:18.
8. See Romans 8:38-39.
9. See John 15:9-10.
10. See 2 Corinthians 10:3-5.
11. Jude 1:24-25.
12. See Jude 1:1.
13. See Romans 10:9.
14. Matthew 28:18-20.

ABOUT THE AUTHORS

Attorney **Mark Hitchcock** thought his career was set after graduating from law school. But after what Mark calls a "clear call to full-time ministry," he changed course and went to Dallas Theological Seminary, completing master's and doctoral degrees. Since 1991, Mark has authored numerous books, serves as senior pastor of Faith Bible Church in Edmond, Oklahoma, and is also an associate professor of Bible exposition at Dallas Theological Seminary. Mark and his wife, Cheryl, live in Edmond with their two sons, Justin and Samuel.

Jeff Kinley empowers people with God's vintage truth through writing and speaking. A bestselling author, Jeff has written twenty-five books. He is a graduate of Dallas Theological Seminary (ThM) and is a frequent speaker at churches across the country. He and his wife live in Arkansas and have three grown sons. See jeffkinley.com for more information about his ministry.

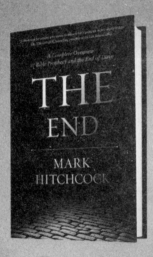
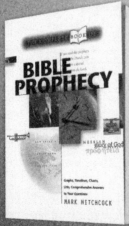
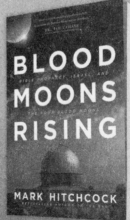

Online Discussion *guide*

TAKE *your* TYNDALE READING
EXPERIENCE *to the* NEXT LEVEL

A FREE discussion guide for this book
is available at bookclubhub.net, perfect
for sparking conversations in your book
group or for digging deeper into the text
on your own.

www.bookclubhub.net

*You'll also find free discussion guides for
other Tyndale books, e-newsletters, e-mail
devotionals, virtual book tours, and more!*